PISA

Education in the Western Balkans

FINDINGS FROM PISA

This work is published under the responsibility of the Secretary-General of the OECD. The opinions expressed and arguments employed herein do not necessarily reflect the official views of OECD member countries.

This document, as well as any data and map included herein, are without prejudice to the status of or sovereignty over any territory, to the delimitation of international frontiers and boundaries and to the name of any territory, city or area.

The statistical data for Israel are supplied by and under the responsibility of the relevant Israeli authorities. The use of such data by the OECD is without prejudice to the status of the Golan Heights, East Jerusalem and Israeli settlements in the West Bank under the terms of international law.

Note by Turkey
The information in this document with reference to "Cyprus" relates to the southern part of the Island. There is no single authority representing both Turkish and Greek Cypriot people on the Island. Turkey recognises the Turkish Republic of Northern Cyprus (TRNC). Until a lasting and equitable solution is found within the context of the United Nations, Turkey shall preserve its position concerning the "Cyprus issue".

Note by all the European Union Member States of the OECD and the European Union
The Republic of Cyprus is recognised by all members of the United Nations with the exception of Turkey. The information in this document relates to the area under the effective control of the Government of the Republic of Cyprus.

Please cite this publication as:
OECD (2020), *Education in the Western Balkans: Findings from PISA*, PISA, OECD Publishing, Paris, https://doi.org/10.1787/764847ff-en.

ISBN 978-92-64-38524-5 (print)
ISBN 978-92-64-43407-3 (pdf)

PISA
ISSN 1990-8539 (print)
ISSN 1996-3777 (online)

Photo credits: Cover © Soloviova Liudmyla/Shutterstock.com; Iakov Filimonov/Shutterstock.com; Rawpixel.com/Shutterstock.com.

Corrigenda to publications may be found on line at: *www.oecd.org/about/publishing/corrigenda.htm*.
© OECD 2020

The use of this work, whether digital or print, is governed by the Terms and Conditions to be found at *http://www.oecd.org/termsandconditions*.

Foreword from the European Commission

In February 2018, the Commission presented the new Western Balkans Strategy, confirming the European future of the region as a geostrategic investment in a stable, strong and united Europe based on common values. This was confirmed at the Zagreb Summit in May this year.

Education, culture, youth and sport, together with research and innovation, are recognised as essential drivers to boost the region's economic development, its competitiveness and social cohesion. This is why I will soon propose a comprehensive Agenda for the Western Balkans on Innovation, Research, Education, Culture, Youth and Sport. This long-term strategy will enhance human capital development and brain circulation, and foster transition to a sustainable and knowledge-based economy.

The strategy will underline the importance of solid evidence when developing inclusive and high quality education and training systems. The outcome of the comparative study in this report will be a crucial step towards the achievement of this objective. It is the result of a joint venture between the European Commission, the OECD and UNICEF, aiming to get maximum value from the 2018 PISA results, which saw the participation of the six Western Balkan countries for the first time.

This joint venture will help the region to identify gaps and develop measures to address its most pressing education needs: reduce the underachievement in basic skills, improve the management of schools, and upgrade teaching methods.

The study takes a special look at home learning and digital competences, just to highlight one success story. I am especially glad to see that digital literacy in the region has steadily improved over the years, with digital skills becoming an essential part of the everyday life of the younger generation.

Enjoy the report.

Commissioner Mariya Gabriel
European Commissioner for Innovation, Research, Culture, Education and Youth

Foreword from UNICEF

If all children are to reach their full potential in life, all children must have an equal chance of receiving a good quality education. The critical importance of education for the prospects and prosperity of individuals, communities and entire nations has been recognised in the global Education 2030 Agenda under the Sustainable Development Goals (SDGs), with SDG 4 demanding inclusive and equitable quality education for all. That goal cannot be met, however, without addressing uneven progress on education. Too often, the most marginalised children are left behind, including girls, ethnic and linguistic minorities, immigrants and refugees, children with disabilities, and those from low-income families or living in remote areas.

If these children are to be fully included in education, we need to understand the factors that inhibit their schooling and exclude them from learning. This new study on the Western Balkan countries aims to fill key knowledge gaps on this issue, carried out jointly by UNICEF, the European Commission (EC) and the Organisation for Economic Co-operation and Development (OECD).

The study is a contribution to the strenuous efforts being made by these countries to introduce reforms that will improve access to quality education and life-long learning, reflecting their firm commitment to the Education 2030 Agenda. It sets out the current education environment and challenges in the Western Balkans to inform data-driven policy and planning that can address the unmet learning needs of children.

Effective policy and practice are illuminated by a knowledge base that is rooted in an in-depth analysis of education systems and the barriers that children face to full inclusion. Drawing on the large-scale data collected by PISA 2018 surveys, the study reveals the underlying challenges in promoting learning and skills development for every child. The analysis also draws on the experiences of children themselves, examining the demographic characteristics of children and their families to provide insights into who is at risk of missing out on education and the need for targeted interventions. A comparative analysis of school systems and teaching practices helps to identify areas that must be addressed to strengthen the capacity of education systems to meet the learning needs of all children. The study could not be more timely, as it sheds light on the preparedness of schools to organise digital learning before the surge in online learning triggered by the COVID-19 crisis.

The study builds on UNICEF's decades of experience in the Western Balkans, working to protect the rights of every child, including their rights to go to school and learn regardless of who they are or where they live. Our goal: to achieve the vision of an inclusive quality education for every child, with equity and learning at its core.

We hope that this study will serve as an evidence base to inform the policies and programmes that are needed to build inclusive and equitable education systems that provide all children with quality learning. UNICEF will continue to listen to the voices of children and work with government, development partners, civil society organisations and the private sector to improve education outcomes for all children; but particularly those who are the most vulnerable.

Afshan Khan
UNICEF Regional Director for Europe and Central Asia
Special Co-ordinator for Refugee and Migrant Response in Europe

Foreword from the OECD

The Western Balkans region has clear aspirations to improve its economic competitiveness and increase the wealth of its citizens. Achieving these aspirations will position it for further integration into Europe, as outlined by the European Commission's Strategy for the Western Balkans. A highly skilled population is integral to creating the dynamic, productive economies that the region desires. This makes developing high quality and equitable education systems, as recognised by the United Nations' Sustainable Development Agenda, critical to the future success of the Western Balkans.

The OECD's Programme for International Student Assessment (PISA) helps countries understand where they stand in terms of their educational outcomes. Results from Western Balkan economies on PISA show that the quality of education in the region has improved over time, though progress can still be made compared to countries in the European Union. Moreover, student outcomes vary greatly between and within education systems in the region; some students are performing very well while others are being left further behind.

Together with the European Commission and United Nations Children's Fund (UNICEF), the OECD is committed to supporting Western Balkan education systems and helping the region achieve its development goals. This comparative study builds upon the long-standing participation of Western Balkan education systems in PISA and the numerous education country reviews conducted by the OECD and UNICEF in the region. We analyse PISA data in detail to identify what the unique features of education in the Western Balkans are and how they might shape student outcomes. Drawing upon our knowledge of education policy and practice in the region, we make recommendations that policy makers can consider when developing future educational reforms.

We hope that this study will not only be a useful resource for education systems in the Western Balkans, but will also further strengthen OECD's ties to the region and its partnership with the European Commission and UNICEF.

Andreas Schleicher
Special Advisor on Education Policy to the Secretary-General
Director for Education and Skills

Table of contents

Foreword from the European Commission — 3

Foreword from UNICEF — 4

Foreword from the OECD — 6

Acronyms and Abbreviations — 10

Executive summary — 11

1 Western Balkan participation and outcomes in PISA 2018 — 15
Education in the Western Balkans — 15
Purpose of this paper and sources of evidence — 15
Key features of Western Balkan economies and their implications for student learning, as measured by PISA — 17
Learning outcomes in the Western Balkans — 23
References — 33
Notes — 34

2 Delivering effective and equitable schooling — 35
Introduction — 35
Student tracking — 35
School resourcing — 45
School networks — 57
References — 62
Notes — 63

3 Assuring high quality teaching — 65
Introduction — 65
Teaching practices — 65
Teacher certification and qualifications — 71
Teacher appraisal and professional development — 76
References — 86
Notes — 87

Tables

Table 1.1. Participation in PISA of Western Balkan education systems — 17
Table 1.2. Socio-economic indicators — 18
Table 1.3. Linguistic populations in Western Balkan education systems — 19
Table 1.4. Duration of compulsory education/training and student age groups, 2018/19 — 20
Table 1.5. Characteristics of the students in the PISA 2018 sample — 22
Table 1.6. Western Balkans PISA performance in reading over time — 23
Table 1.7. Summary description of the eight levels of reading proficiency in PISA 2018 — 26
Table 2.1. Criteria for admission into upper-secondary schools — 36
Table 2.2. External assessments and examinations in the Western Balkans — 43
Table 2.3. Education system funding — 45
Table 2.4. Principals' perceptions of key educational resources — 48
Table 2.5. Principals' perceptions of technological infrastructure — 52
Table 2.6. Principals' perceptions of technological infrastructure in advantaged and disadvantaged schools — 54
Table 2.7. School resources and reading performance — 55
Table 2.8. Changes in demographic indicators from 2000 to 2018 — 57
Table 2.9. Relationship between school network characteristics and student performance in reading — 60
Table 3.1. Indices of teacher practice — 66
Table 3.2. Teacher standards in the Western Balkans — 70
Table 3.3. Requirements to become a fully certified teacher in the Western Balkans — 71

Figures

Figure 1.1. Performance in reading, mathematics and science in Western Balkan education systems, 2018 — 24
Figure 1.2. Mean reading performance and per-capita GDP — 25
Figure 1.3. Proficiency levels in reading of students from Western Balkan education systems — 27
Figure 1.4. Meta-cognitive skills in reading — 28
Figure 1.5. Socio-economic status and student performance — 29
Figure 1.6. Low-achieving students and educational programmes — 30
Figure 1.7. Differences in reading performance by gender over time — 31
Figure 1.8. Performance in reading by language of instruction — 32
Figure 2.1. Academic selectivity into upper secondary schools in international education systems — 37
Figure 2.2. Increased likelihood of attending a vocational programme according to gender and socio-economic status — 38
Figure 2.3. Performance differences between general education and vocational students — 39
Figure 2.4. Difference in student performance between students in different grades in general education and vocational programmes — 40
Figure 2.5. Student behaviour in general education and vocational programmes — 41
Figure 2.6. Differences in expectations between students who attend general education and vocational programmes — 44
Figure 2.7. Cumulative spending through age 15 and relationship with performance — 46
Figure 2.8. Principals' perceptions of material resources in advantaged and disadvantaged schools — 49
Figure 2.9. Principals' perceptions of material resources in general and vocational schools — 50
Figure 2.10. Technological infrastructure — 51
Figure 2.11. Technological infrastructure in advantaged and disadvantaged schools — 53
Figure 2.12. School size across the Western Balkans — 58
Figure 2.13. Student-teacher ratios — 59
Figure 3.1. Teacher practices — 67
Figure 3.2. Teacher practices and reading performance — 68
Figure 3.3. Teacher behaviours and practices that may hinder student instruction — 69
Figure 3.4. Teacher qualifications — 72
Figure 3.5. Teacher qualifications and student outcomes in reading — 73
Figure 3.6. Teacher qualifications and teacher practices — 74
Figure 3.7. Using student assessment to appraise teachers — 77
Figure 3.8. Professional development and teacher practices — 78
Figure 3.9. Professional development — 79
Figure 3.10. Professional development for teachers in schools with more advantaged and disadvantaged students — 80

Figure 3.11. Teacher participation in professional development according to their languages of instruction   81
Figure 3.12. Teacher practices in general education and vocational schools   83
Figure 3.13. Teacher practices in advantaged and disadvantaged schools   84

Boxes

Box 1.1. Areas for further analysis   16
Box 1.2. Meta-cognitive skills   27
Box 2.1. Student behaviour in general education and vocational programmes   40
Box 2.2. Strengthening the value of vocational education   44
Box 3.1. Teaching practices in general education and vocational schools, and in advantaged and disadvantaged schools   83

Acronyms and Abbreviations

CEEC	Central and Eastern European Countries
ESCS	PISA index of Economic, Social and Cultural Status
EU	European Union
GDP	Gross Domestic Product
ITE	Initial Teacher Education
PISA	Programme for International Student Assessment
PPP	Purchasing Power Parity
UNICEF	United Nations Children's Fund
USD	United States dollars
VET	Vocational education and training

Executive summary

The Western Balkans region (defined by the European Union as Albania, Bosnia and Herzegovina, Kosovo, Montenegro, the Republic of North Macedonia and Serbia) is undergoing a period of rapid economic transition. Despite achieving considerable progress, however, the region is struggling to attain the same level of development as many of its neighbours, with per-capita gross domestic product being lower and youth unemployment rates being higher than most countries in Central and Eastern Europe. A knowledgeable and skilled population is an indispensable component to the dynamic economies and inclusive, cohesive societies that the Western Balkans aspire to build, which makes education reform a central pillar of regional development efforts.

To better understand learning outcomes and benchmark their education systems, Western Balkan economies have continuously participated in the OECD's Programme for International Student Assessment (PISA), and did so simultaneously for the first time in 2018. This paper analyses PISA 2018 data to help determine what 15-year-olds in the Western Balkans know and can do. Based upon these findings, and drawing upon an international knowledge base that includes several OECD-UNICEF policy reviews, this paper also suggests policy considerations about how education systems in the region can improve schooling and teaching to help all students learn and succeed.

Learning outcomes

Results from PISA 2018 reveal that overall outcomes from the region are improving. All systems that participated in PISA prior to 2015 raised their performance in 2018 while also testing a greater share of 15-year-old students, demonstrating that educational improvement and expansion are not mutually exclusive. Nevertheless, performance in the Western Balkans (average score in reading, 402) is generally lower than that of countries across Central and Eastern European Countries (CEEC) (476)[1], the European Union (EU) (481), and the OECD (487). Achievement within the region also varies, with Kosovo scoring 353 in reading and Serbia scoring 440.

Worryingly, PISA 2018 results show that learning outcomes in the region are highly inequitable. Boys perform worse than girls at rates exceeding international averages. In systems with linguistic minorities, learning gaps between linguistic student groups can be greater than 70 points in reading. Compared to students enrolled in general upper-secondary programmes, students enrolled in vocational programmes underperform to larger degrees than across OECD countries.

Delivering effective and equitable schooling

The educational outcomes of the Western Balkans region can be partly explained by policies related to schooling. Enrolment into upper-secondary education is very academically selective when compared to international benchmarks, and the difference in achievement between students in different tracks reflects that selectivity. Nevertheless, evidence from PISA suggests that how regional systems assess students, which then influences how they track students, might capture students' backgrounds (i.e. their gender and socio-economic status) in addition to their abilities. This finding raises questions about the fairness of student tracking decisions, especially given the size of vocational sectors in the region (which are much larger than vocational sectors in OECD and EU countries), the lack of permeability between tracks and the extent to which a student's upper-secondary track can shape their future success. Education systems in the region are addressing these issues by improving student assessment practices, in particular by introducing standardised, national assessments that can provide external validation of student learning and can help teachers improve their own judgements.

Another unique feature of Western Balkan education systems is their level and distribution of school resources. Compared to international benchmarks, education spending in the region is low, especially when considering the significant infrastructural investment that many schools need. In addition, spending is inequitable. Schools with more socio-economically advantaged student intakes tend to enjoy greater resourcing than schools with more disadvantaged student intakes, which can contribute to inequitable learning outcomes. Western Balkan systems can consider several strategies to address these concerns, such as establishing re-distributive resourcing policies and strengthening school evaluation to better identify the needs of schools.

Finally, Western Balkan systems, like many around the world, are confronting issues related to demographic changes, such as declining birth rates and increasing urbanisation. These issues include overcrowded schools in urban areas, and shrinking schools in rural areas that can sometimes have more staff than students. This situation is leading to inefficient resource allocation in some cases, which exacerbates existing concerns about inadequate and inequitable resourcing. Rationalising school networks might help consolidate resources where they are needed most, though policy makers should take care to ensure that all students still have access to appropriate educational services.

Assuring high quality teaching

Teaching is one of the most important factors of an education system and can significantly shape student learning. In the Western Balkans, teacher practices are largely traditional and centred around the teacher (e.g. delivering a lecture to the whole class), with less emphasis on individualised, adaptive instruction (which is associated with higher student outcomes) compared to international benchmarks. These circumstances might also contribute to inequities in learning, as teachers might not instruct students from diverse backgrounds in ways that best help them learn. To improve the situation, Western Balkan systems have developed teacher standards that spell out how teachers are expected to teach. Using these standards to help determine career progression and professional development can further encourage teachers to implement the desired practices in their classrooms.

Requirements related to certification and qualifications can help ensure high quality teaching. Like most teachers in OECD and EU countries, most teachers in the Western Balkans are fully certified, though fewer hold master's degrees. Unlike international benchmarks, however, teacher certification and advanced qualifications are not positively associated with increased student performance or improved teacher practices, suggesting that these quality assurance mechanisms are not always fulfilling their purposes. To address this issue, Western Balkan systems can consider introducing consistent and rigorous accreditation criteria for initial teacher education providers, along with aligning certification requirements, such as examinations, with the practical demands of the job.

To improve teacher practice, many education systems appraise teachers to identify their needs and then offer them relevant professional development. In the Western Balkans, teacher appraisal differs from international benchmarks by relying heavily upon student assessment results. This practice does not accurately capture the extent to which teachers help all students learn and could incentivise teachers to focus their attentions on the highest performing students. Regarding professional development, teachers in the region participate at rates comparable to international benchmarks, but do so inequitably. Teachers who teach in schools with more advantaged students usually participate more than teachers who teach in schools with more disadvantaged students. Worryingly, more professional development in the region, unlike in OECD countries, is not associated with more frequent use of desired teaching practices. To strengthen teacher appraisal, education systems in the region can consider adopting a more holistic approach to teacher appraisal, such as by de-emphasising student assessment results and relying more on classroom observations and reviewing teacher portfolios. Western Balkan systems might expand the availability of professional development by considering digital training options so more teachers can access the opportunities, and strengthen the quality of professional development by introducing accreditation of training providers.

Notes

[1] The OECD considers CEEC to be composed of Albania, Bulgaria, Croatia, the Czech Republic, Estonia, Hungary, Latvia, Lithuania, Poland, Romania, the Slovak Republic and Slovenia. For this paper, results that represent the CEEC average are calculated without data from Albania to avoid overlap with results that represent the Western Balkans average.

1 Western Balkan participation and outcomes in PISA 2018

Education in the Western Balkans

The turn of the new millennium marked a period of stability and economic progress in Eastern Europe, with many countries from the area experiencing record growth and joining the European Union (EU). However, the six economies of the Western Balkans[1] (Albania, Bosnia and Herzegovina, North Macedonia, Montenegro, Kosovo and Serbia) have struggled to achieve the same level of social and economic development as many neighbouring countries. Notably, the region's average per-capita gross domestic product (GDP) remains much lower than that of Central and Eastern European Countries (CEEC)[2] and unemployment rates, especially among youth, are very high in many parts of the Western Balkans (Table 1.2). Economies in the region have introduced reforms to improve their competitiveness and strengthen governance, motivated in part by the eventual goal of EU membership.

Education is a central pillar of regional reform efforts as knowledge and skilled populations are considered crucial for building dynamic economies and inclusive, cohesive societies. The Western Balkans have achieved near universal access to primary and lower secondary schooling, but participation rates of upper-secondary completion are below EU standards and the quality and relevance of learning is an increasing concern. In response, economies in the region have introduced competence-based curricula, adopted professional standards for teachers and established school evaluation frameworks in attempts to modernise the instructional system and better equip young people with the skills they need to succeed. However, these reforms, while sometimes contributing to overall improvement, are not benefitting all population groups equitably and large shares of students continue to leave school without mastering important basic competences. Addressing these challenges will be crucial to the region's economic development, social prosperity and integration into Europe.

Purpose of this paper and sources of evidence

The pivot of Western Balkan economies towards the EU and their focus on improving education have contributed to their increased engagement in international educational activities. A key part of this engagement is participation in the OECD's Programme for International Student Assessment (PISA), which benchmarks the performance of education systems around the world. Western Balkan economies have participated in PISA since 2000 and all six economies participated together for the first time in 2018. Moreover, over the past two years, four Western Balkan economies have completed or are participating in OECD policy reviews of their educational evaluation and assessment systems, conducted in collaboration with the United Nations Children's Fund (UNICEF). These activities have generated a rich knowledge base about education in the Western Balkans (OECD, 2019[1]; Maghnouj et al., 2019[2]; Maghnouj et al., 2020[3]).

This paper uses PISA data, policy findings from OECD-UNICEF country reviews and international research to identify strengths and challenges that are common to Western Balkan education systems (some issues are only relevant to some systems, which is further explained in Box 1.1). Such a multi-country analysis can help determine regionally relevant practices that can lead to improved student outcomes, particularly in secondary school (PISA primarily collects data at the secondary level).

> ### Box 1.1. Areas for further analysis
>
> This paper focuses on insights from PISA that can help inform the most salient and common educational challenges facing the Western Balkans. In developing this paper, several areas were identified that might benefit from further analysis, but are not addressed here because they do not concern all education systems in the region. For instance, PISA results typically highlight differences between public and private schools. However, the region's private school sectors are small. Only Albania's share of private school students who participated in PISA was greater than 3%. Similarly, PISA focuses on the differences in outcomes between non-immigrant and immigrant students[3], who represent 13% of PISA-participating students across the OECD and 12% across the EU. However, only 4% of students in the Western Balkans have an immigrant background and only in Serbia do immigrants comprise a share of the student population greater than 6%. Therefore, while these issues may be important in some systems, they are not significant factors to the overall performance of the region. However, it is nevertheless important to understand these issues systemically, such as the capacity of schools to support diverse students where they are concentrated. Many Western Balkan economies have prepared national reports of their PISA 2018 results, which address these and other issues that are pertinent to their specific contexts.
>
> Other issues might be important in the region, but are not captured by PISA data. Students with disabilities, for example, are excluded from the PISA sample. Identifying different ethnic groups, in particular the Roma, is not available in PISA and therefore results cannot be directly disaggregated according to this dimension. However, in the section about Performance and equity, ethnicity is explored through the language of testing.

Participation in PISA

PISA is a triennial survey (due to the COVID-19 epidemic, PISA will be offered next in 2022) of 15-year old students around the world that assesses the extent to which they have acquired the knowledge and skills in reading, mathematics and science that are essential for full participation in social and economic life. PISA assessments do not just ascertain whether students can reproduce what they have been taught; they examine how well students can extrapolate from what they have learned and apply their knowledge in real life settings. Through questionnaires, PISA also collects information about the educational contexts of countries, which, when analysed alongside student performance, provides useful insights about what impacts student learning around the world.

Albania and North Macedonia took part in the very first administration of PISA in 2000; Serbia in 2003; Montenegro in 2006; Kosovo in PISA 2015, and Bosnia and Herzegovina in PISA 2018 (Table 1.1). All economies in the region, except North Macedonia, have also transitioned to the computer-based assessment, which allows them to assess students using technologically enhanced items (e.g. conducting experiments) that were specifically developed for PISA 2018. The computer-based version also enabled access to many of the new questionnaire items (e.g. some questions about teacher practices). It will be important that Western Balkan economies continue to participate in PISA; as Table 1.1 indicates, the region's engagement so far has been inconsistent over cycles, which has limited the monitoring of trends and comparisons both within and across economies.

All countries and economies in PISA 2018 distributed the student and school questionnaires. Some participants also administered optional background questionnaires. These included up to four additional questionnaires for students (about their educational careers, information and communication technology (ICT) familiarity, well-being and financial literacy); an optional questionnaire for parents; and an optional questionnaire for teachers. Table 1.1 also shows the optional questionnaires taken by Western Balkan economies in PISA 2018.

Table 1.1. Participation in PISA of Western Balkan education systems

Participation in PISA cycles		Albania	Bosnia and Herzegovina	Kosovo	Montenegro	North Macedonia	Serbia
PISA 2000		X				X	
PISA 2003							X
PISA 2006					X		X
PISA 2009		X			X		X
PISA 2012		X			X		X
PISA 2015		X		X	X	X	
PISA 2018		X	X	X	X	X	X

Features of participation in PISA 2018		Albania	Bosnia and Herzegovina	Kosovo	Montenegro	North Macedonia	Serbia
Computer format of the assessment		X	X	X	X		X
Global Competence assessment		X					X
Financial Literacy assessment and questionnaire							X
Educational Career		X					X
Optional questionnaires	ICT	X					X
	Parent						
	Teacher	X					
	Well-being						X
Languages of the assessment		Albanian	Bosnian, Croatian, Serbian	Albanian	Albanian, Montenegrin	Macedonian, Albanian	Hungarian, Serbian

StatLink https://doi.org/10.1787/888934199539

Country reviews

The OECD has conducted policy reviews of most OECD and EU countries, as well as an increasing number of partner economies. These reviews draw on evidence, including PISA data, to examine key education policy issues with a strong focus on improving the quality and equity of student learning outcomes. In the Western Balkans, the OECD has recently completed education policy reviews in partnership with UNICEF for North Macedonia (2019), Serbia (2020) and Albania (2020), with an ongoing review of Bosnia and Herzegovina, which is expected to be completed in 2021. These studies focus on policies related to evaluation and assessment, recognising that policies in the areas of student assessment, teacher appraisal, and school and system evaluation provide powerful levers for transforming school quality. This paper draws on the knowledge base built from these reviews to situate PISA findings from the Western Balkans within the educational context of the region.

Key features of Western Balkan economies and their implications for student learning, as measured by PISA

In each participating economy, PISA 2018 assessed a representative sample of children between the ages of 15 years and 3 months and 16 years and 2 months who were enrolled in an educational institution at grade 7 or above. A two-stage sampling procedure selected a representative sample of at least 150 schools and roughly 42 students within each of those schools. The majority of economies, including those in the Western Balkans, assessed between 5 000 and 7 000 students. The national context of each economy that participates in PISA affects greatly the students who are sampled to participate in the survey. This section discusses some of the key features of Western Balkan education systems, and how these contexts are represented in their PISA 2018 student samples (Table 1.5).

Socio-economic context

Western Balkan education systems have more socio-economically disadvantaged students compared to OECD countries

An important concern for all countries is how students from disadvantaged backgrounds perform compared to their advantaged peers, which helps indicate the extent to which the school system helps students overcome socio-economic inequalities. Economies in the Western Balkans are, on average, lower income than those in the EU and OECD. For example, the Western Balkans had an average GDP per-capita of 15 749 (PPP, USD) in 2018, which was much lower than the OECD average of roughly 45 624.

While wealth is an important measure of socio-economic status, other factors also influence a student's level of advantage. To capture more of these factors, in PISA, a student's socio-economic background is represented through the index of economic, social and cultural status (ESCS), which is created based upon information about a student's home environment, parents' level of education and parents' employment. This index is calculated such that the OECD average is 0.0. The EU average is also 0.0 and the CEEC average is -0.1. The average ESCS across the Western Balkans is -0.4, which is consistent with economic data that suggests students in the region are generally more disadvantaged. There are disparities within the region, however. Serbia has an ESCS of -0.2, while Albania has an average ESCS of -0.9 (Table 1.2). Since socio-economic context and student performance are closely related, it is important to consider these data when interpreting and comparing the educational outcomes of the Western Balkans (see the section on Performance and equity).

Table 1.2. Socio-economic indicators

	Per-capita GDP in 2018 (PPP, USD)	PISA 2018 ESCS
Albania	13 364	-0,9
Bosnia and Herzegovina	14 624	-0,6
Kosovo	11 384	-0,5
Montenegro	20 690	-0,2
North Macedonia	16 359	-0,3
Serbia	17 435	-0,2
Western Balkans average	15 749	-0,4
CEEC average	32 132	-0,1
EU average	43 738	0,0
OECD average	45 624	0,0

Sources: The World Bank (n.d.[4]). GDP per-capita (current US$). https://data.worldbank.org/indicator/NY.GDP.PCAP.PP.CD (accessed 11 January 2020).
OECD (2019[5]). PISA 2018 Database. https://www.oecd.org/pisa/data/2018database/ (accessed 17 November 2020).

Schools in the Western Balkans are located in different settings, though the small geographic size of some economies limits analysis of schooling in rural areas

Around the world, schools in urban areas tend to have more resources and provide higher quality education than schools in rural areas, though some systems are more effective in mitigating these disparities than others (Echazarra and Radinger, 2019[6]). It is, therefore, important to understand the differences in outcomes between students who attend urban schools compared to students who attend rural schools. As part of the school questionnaire completed by school principals, PISA asks principals to identify the size of the community in which their schools are located. Rural areas are communities of less than 3 000 people, towns 3 000 to 100 000 people and cities (urban areas) more than 100 000 people.

The share of students enrolled in schools located in rural areas, towns and cities is similar on average across Western Balkans economies, the EU and the OECD (less than 10% in rural areas; more than half in towns; and about a third in cities). However, there are wide variations across education systems in the Western Balkans. In Montenegro, North Macedonia and Serbia, no 15-year-old student in the PISA sample was enrolled in a rural school. By contrast, in Kosovo and Albania 13% and 26% of students attended a rural school, respectively. These differences do not necessarily mean that Montenegro, North Macedonia and Serbia do not have rural communities, but rather that their education systems might construct upper-secondary schools in larger communities and transport students from more rural areas to attend those schools. Care should be taken when making inferences about the results based on geographic factors.

Western Balkan economies are ethnically diverse

The presence of different ethnic groups in several Western Balkan economies has important policy implications. While PISA 2018 does not ask specifically about student ethnicity, it does identify students' linguistic backgrounds and this paper explores that dimension, whenever relevant and possible, to learn more about economies' education policies related to ethnic groups and multilingual schooling.

In all Western Balkan systems except Albania and Kosovo there is more than one language of instruction (see Table 1.3). The number of students who learn in different languages, however, and how their school systems accommodate their needs, varies across economies. In North Macedonia, where around 23% of the population is Albanian, the education system ensures that the same curriculum is delivered through mother tongue instruction at all levels (OECD, 2019[1]). In Bosnia and Herzegovina, distinct school systems within the country educate students in different languages and according to different policies and curricula.

Table 1.3. Linguistic populations in Western Balkan education systems

Share of PISA-participating students who attend school in various languages

Bosnia and Herzegovina	Bosnian (56%)
	Serbian (32%)
	Croatian (12%)
Montenegro	Montenegrin (96%)
	Albanian (4%)
North Macedonia	Macedonian (73%)
	Albanian (27%)

Note: In Serbia, less than 2% of the 15-year-old population attend school in Hungarian. These results are not shown because the sample size is too small to make meaningful inferences.
Source: OECD (2019[5]). PISA 2018 Database. https://www.oecd.org/pisa/data/2018database/ (accessed 17 November 2020).

Educational landscape

Students in the Western Balkans typically take PISA in grades 9 and 10

The modal grade (the most common grade) of students who participate in PISA varies depending on the structure of each education system. In Bosnia and Herzegovina, Montenegro, North Macedonia and Serbia, almost all 15-year-old students are enrolled in the first year of upper-secondary education. In Albania and Kosovo comparatively more are still in lower-secondary education.

The modal grade also affects the population sampled in PISA. By definition, only 15-year-olds who are enrolled in schools can participate. In countries where the modal grade is after the last grade of compulsory education, the population that is eligible to be in the PISA sample can be considerably lower than the overall population of 15-year-olds (a ratio referred to as the coverage index). In Azerbaijan (Baku), where compulsory education ends at age 15, the PISA-eligible sample of 15-year-olds only represented 46% of all 15-year-olds, compared to almost 100% in Germany, where compulsory education extends to age 18. In the Western Balkans, education is generally compulsory to the end of lower-secondary school (Table 1.4). Depending on when students begin school, the coverage index ranges from 76% of 15 year olds in Albania to 95% of 15-year-olds in Montenegro. Readers of this paper should interpret PISA results in light of these differences in coverage.

Table 1.4. Duration of compulsory education/training and student age groups, 2018/19

	Starting age in ISCED 1 (2011)	General leaving age	Grade that corresponds to end of compulsory education
Albania	6	15	Grade 9
Bosnia and Herzegovina	6	15	Grade 9
Kosovo	Data not available	Data not available	Data not available
Montenegro	6	15	Grade 9
North Macedonia	6	15	Grade 9
Serbia	6.5	14.5	Grade 8

Notes: Grade that corresponds to end of compulsory education is from OECD-UNICEF country reviews.
Starting age refers to the official age at which students start compulsory education/training.
The possibility of early entry to primary education is not taken into account nor are the specific admission conditions of pupils officially recognised with special educational needs.
Leaving age refers to the statutory age at which students are expected to complete compulsory education/training.
Sources: European Commission/EACEA/Eurydice (2018[7]). Compulsory Education in Europe – 2018/19.

Western Balkan education systems track students into general and vocational programmes in upper-secondary school

Many countries divide students into different types of educational programmes, or tracks. Among these programmes, the two most common are general education, which typically prepares students for academic tertiary studies, and vocational education, which equips students with practical skills to enter the workforce while also keeping the door open to tertiary education. Countries vary in terms of when students are selected into different tracks. While some systems, such as Germany, start sorting students after primary education, the majority start offering distinct tracks to students at the end of lower-secondary school.

The permeability of education tracks also varies across education systems. In the United States, for example, vocational and general education students might attend the same school, be eligible to take each other's courses and even switch their tracks. In the Netherlands, vocational and general education students generally attend separate schools, study separate curricula and cannot easily switch tracks. Finally, the extent to which students in different educational tracks are eligible for future opportunities also varies. In Georgia, for example, vocational upper-secondary graduates are ineligible to enrol in academic tertiary programmes. Across the OECD, countries have moved to introduce more flexible policies, which keep a range of tertiary options available to graduates of vocational education and training (VET) tracks as a means of avoiding dead ends and encouraging higher levels of foundational skills development (OECD, 2010[8]).

In the Western Balkans, students are tracked into general education and vocational programmes at the upper-secondary level. Several features about tracking in the Western Balkans are distinctive. First, the vocational sectors in Western Balkans education systems are much larger than international benchmarks. On average across the region, 59% of PISA-participating students were enrolled in vocational schools, compared to much lower shares in CEEC (23%), EU (17%) and OECD (12%) countries. Within the region, the share of PISA-participating students from vocational schools ranges from 72% in Serbia, to 7% in Albania. It should be noted, however, that these figures are influenced by the grade when students enter upper-secondary school vis-à-vis the grades represented in the PISA sample. In Kosovo, upper-secondary education begins in grade 10, which is the first year students can enrol in a vocational education programme. If only considering 15-year-old students in grade 10, the share of PISA participants attending vocational schools in Kosovo rises by 12 percentage points (Table 1.5). For this reason, many analyses in this paper that focus on educational tracks focus only on students from upper-secondary schools.

Furthermore, education tracks in the Western Balkans are not permeable. Vocational and general education programmes are typically located in separate school buildings and students cannot change their programme of study or take select courses from one while being enrolled in the other. However, after completing upper-secondary education, students from either programme are eligible to enrol in four-year bachelor's programmes. It is important to consider these features when drawing conclusions about the motivations and outcomes of students in the Western Balkans.

Table 1.5. Characteristics of the students in the PISA 2018 sample

	Albania	Bosnia and Herzegovina	Kosovo	Montenegro	North Macedonia	Serbia	Western Balkans average	CEEC average	EU average	OECD average
Number of students	6 359	6 480	5 058	6 666	5 569	6 609	-	-	-	-
Percentage of the 15-year-old population covered by the PISA sample (Coverage Index 3)	76	82	84	95	95	89	87	88	90	88
Modal grade	Grade 10	Grade 10	Grade 10	Grade 10	Grade 10	Grade 9	-	-	-	-
Percentage in upper-secondary school	62	84	76	97	100	99	86	-	-	-
ESCS	-0.9	-0.6	-0.5	-0.2	-0.3	-0.2	-0.4	-0.1	0.0	0.0
Percentage of girls	49	49	50	48	48	49	49	50	49	50
Percentage of students with an immigrant background	1	3	1	6	2	9	4	4	12	13
Percentage of students who speak the test language at home	96	94	97	96	93	95	95	93	84	88
Percentage of students in private schools	11	1	1	0	1	3	3	6	18	1
Percentage of students enrolled in the following programmes: General or modular programmes (overall/upper-secondary school)	93/89	34/21	60/48	35/33	41/41	28/28	41/43	77	83	88
Vocational programmes (overall/upper-secondary school)	7/11	66/79	40/52	65/67	59/59	72/72	59/57	23 (overall)	17 (overall)	12 (overall)
Percentage of students enrolled in schools located in: A village or rural areas (fewer than 3 000 people)	26	7	13	0	0	0	8	13	9	9
Towns (from 3 000 to about 100 000 people)	38	72	62	67	54	51	57	56	62	53
Cities (over 100 000 people)	36	22	25	32	46	49	35	31	29	38

Source: OECD (2019[5]). PISA 2018 Database. https://www.oecd.org/pisa/data/2018database/ (accessed 17 November 2020).

StatLink https://doi.org/10.1787/888934199558

Learning outcomes in the Western Balkans

Overall performance

PISA results[4] show that student outcomes in Western Balkan economies have generally improved in the last two decades. Most education systems in the region have also increased their coverage indices at the same time, showing that gains in educational access and learning are not mutually exclusive (Table 1.6).

Table 1.6. Western Balkans PISA performance in reading over time

	Score points in first year of participation	Score points in 2018	Coverage index in earliest year of availability	Coverage index in 2018
Albania	**349 (2000)**	**405**	61% (2009)	76%
Bosnia and Herzegovina	-	403	-	82%
Kosovo	347 (2015)	353	71% (2015)	84%
Montenegro	**392 (2006)**	**421**	84% (2006)	95%
North Macedonia	**373 (2000)**	**393**	95% (2015)	95%
Serbia	**401 (2006)**	**439**	83% (2006)	88%

Notes: Statistically significant performance differences are represented in bold.
Coverage index refers to the percentage of 15 year olds that are represented in a country's PISA sample.
Data for the coverage index is not available before 2003.
Source: OECD (2019[5]). PISA 2018 Database. https://www.oecd.org/pisa/data/2018database/ (accessed 17 November 2020).

However, while the performance of Western Balkan education systems has improved, outcomes in the region are still lower than international benchmarks. In PISA 2018, students from the Western Balkans scored, on average, 402 points in reading, 414 points in mathematics and 408 in science, meaning that about 80% of students across OECD countries scored higher than the average student in the region (Figure 1.1). However, there are large differences between education systems within the Western Balkans. Serbia's average scores in reading, mathematics and science, for instance, are close to those of some countries in the European Union, such as Bulgaria, Greece and Romania. On the other hand, Kosovo's average performance is closer to that of lower-middle income countries like Indonesia and Morocco.

Figure 1.1. Performance in reading, mathematics and science in Western Balkan education systems, 2018

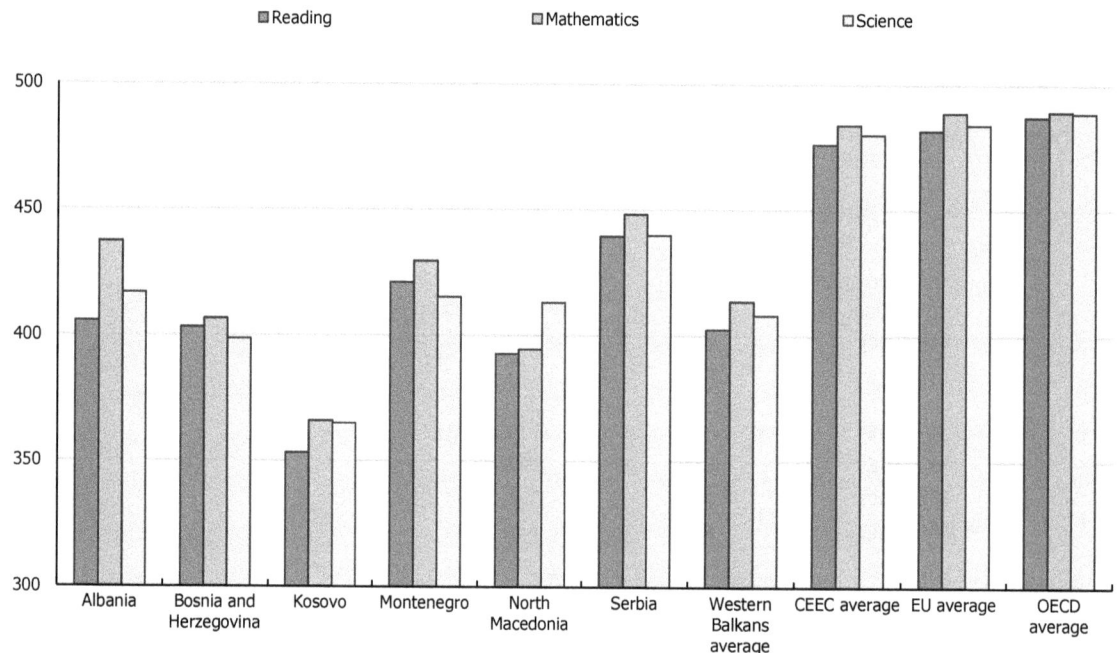

Source: OECD (2019[5]). PISA 2018 Database. https://www.oecd.org/pisa/data/2018database/ (accessed 17 November 2020), Tables I.B1.4, I.B1.5 and I.B1.6.

StatLink https://doi.org/10.1787/888934199577

As mentioned, it is important to interpret PISA results in light of participants' economic development, as 44% of performance differences in mean reading scores between countries in PISA 2018 can be accounted for by national income (OECD, 2019[9]). Figure 1.2 shows the performance of education systems relative to their per-capita GDP. In general, education systems in the Western Balkans perform around what would be predicted by their levels of economic development. However, the higher outcomes among some countries and economies relative to others with similar income levels signals the potential for policy to help overcome resource constraints.

Figure 1.2. Mean reading performance and per-capita GDP

Source: OECD (2019[5]), PISA 2018 Database, https://www.oecd.org/pisa/data/2018database/ (accessed 17 November 2020). Tables I.B1.4 and B3.1.4.

StatLink https://doi.org/10.1787/888934028387

To help understand differences in student knowledge and skills, PISA categorises student performance into a range of eight proficiency levels. These levels range from the highest (Level 6) to the lowest (Level 1c) proficiency (Table 1.7). In 2018, Level 1c was added to the PISA proficiency scale to provide more information on the capabilities of low-achieving students, which are defined as having scored below the baseline level of proficiency (i.e. below Level 2) needed to fully participate in modern societies.

Table 1.7. Summary description of the eight levels of reading proficiency in PISA 2018

Level	Lower score limit	Percentage of students able to perform tasks at each level or above (OECD average)	Characteristics of tasks
6	698	1.3%	Readers at Level 6 can comprehend lengthy and abstract texts in which the information of interest is deeply embedded and only indirectly related to the task. They can compare, contrast and integrate information representing multiple and potentially conflicting perspectives, using multiple criteria and generating inferences across distant pieces of information to determine how the information may be used.
5	626	8.7%	Readers at Level 5 can comprehend lengthy texts, inferring which information in the text is relevant even though the information of interest may be easily overlooked. They can perform causal or other forms of reasoning based on a deep understanding of extended pieces of text. They can also answer indirect questions by inferring the relationship between the question and one or several pieces of information distributed within or across multiple texts and sources, and can establish distinctions between content and purpose, and between fact and opinion.
4	553	27.6%	At Level 4, readers can comprehend extended passages in single or multiple-text settings. They interpret the meaning of nuances of language in a section of text by taking into account the text as a whole. In other interpretative tasks, students demonstrate understanding and application of ad hoc categories. They can compare perspectives and draw inferences based on multiple sources.
3	480	53.6%	Readers at Level 3 can represent the literal meaning of single or multiple texts in the absence of explicit content or organisational clues. Readers can integrate content and generate both basic and more advanced inferences. They can also integrate several parts of a piece of text in order to identify the main idea, understand a relationship or construe the meaning of a word or phrase when the required information is featured on a single page.
2	407	77.4%	Readers at Level 2 can identify the main idea in a piece of text of moderate length. They can understand relationships or construe meaning within a limited part of the text when the information is not prominent by producing basic inferences, and/or when the text(s) include some distracting information.
1a	335	92.3%	Readers at Level 1a can understand the literal meaning of sentences or short passages. Readers at this level can also recognise the main theme or the author's purpose in a piece of text about a familiar topic, and make a simple connection between several adjacent pieces of information, or between the given information and their own prior knowledge.
1b	262	98.6%	Readers at Level 1b can evaluate the literal meaning of simple sentences. They can also interpret the literal meaning of texts by making simple connections between adjacent pieces of information in the question and/or the text.
1c	189	99.9%	Readers at Level 1c can understand and affirm the meaning of short, syntactically simple sentences on a literal level, and read for a clear and simple purpose within a limited amount of time.

Source: OECD (2019[5]). PISA 2018 Database. https://www.oecd.org/pisa/data/2018database/ (accessed 17 November 2020).

Approximately 46% of students on average across Western Balkan school systems scored above the baseline level of proficiency in reading (Figure 1.3). In comparison, 77% of students on average across OECD countries, and 76% across EU countries, scored above the baseline level. Worryingly, there are very few students in the region who have mastered the most sophisticated higher order skills and are well positioned to drive economic growth in the future (Box 1.2). Economies will struggle to develop without the type of human capital that these students represent.

Figure 1.3. Proficiency levels in reading of students from Western Balkan education systems

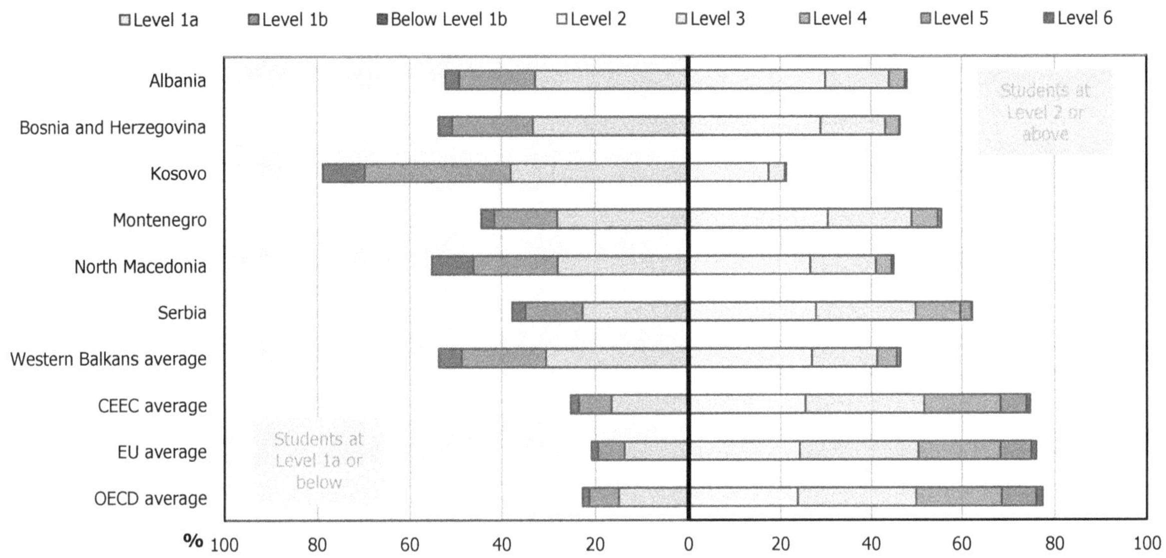

Note: Since North Macedonia took the paper-based version of PISA, Level 1c of reading proficiency cannot be reliably calculated. In order to make results comparable, results for all systems are presented starting from Level 1b.
Source: OECD (2019[5]), PISA 2018 Database. https://www.oecd.org/pisa/data/2018database/ (accessed 17 November 2020). Tables I.B1.1.

StatLink https://doi.org/10.1787/888934199596

Box 1.2. Meta-cognitive skills

In addition to measuring students' reading literacy in general, PISA 2018 measured a specific set of reading skills, called meta-cognitive skills. PISA 2018 defines meta-cognitive skills as knowing how to guide one's own understanding and learn in different contexts (OECD, 2019[10]). Having meta-cognitive skills is crucial in modern societies because they help individuals navigate, interpret and solve unanticipated problems. To measure meta-cognitive skills, PISA asked students about the usefulness of various strategies (understanding and remembering; summarising; assessing credibility) for accomplishing different types of reading tasks and compared their responses to those given by a group of experts. All education systems in the Western Balkans are below the OECD, EU and CEEC averages in terms of students' meta-cognitive skills (Figure 1.4). Students in the region struggle most when asked to choose the best strategies for assessing the credibility of a source. For example, PISA asked students what is an appropriate response to receiving an email from a mobile phone operator informing them that they have won a smartphone. Western Balkan students were more likely to say that clicking on the associated link and filling out an online form was appropriate. Students from OECD countries were more likely to be sceptical of such an offer, saying that they would check the website of the mobile phone operator to see if the offer is mentioned or delete the email without clicking on the link. This finding has economic and social implications, as it suggests that students from the region might be less discerning and critical of the information that they access.

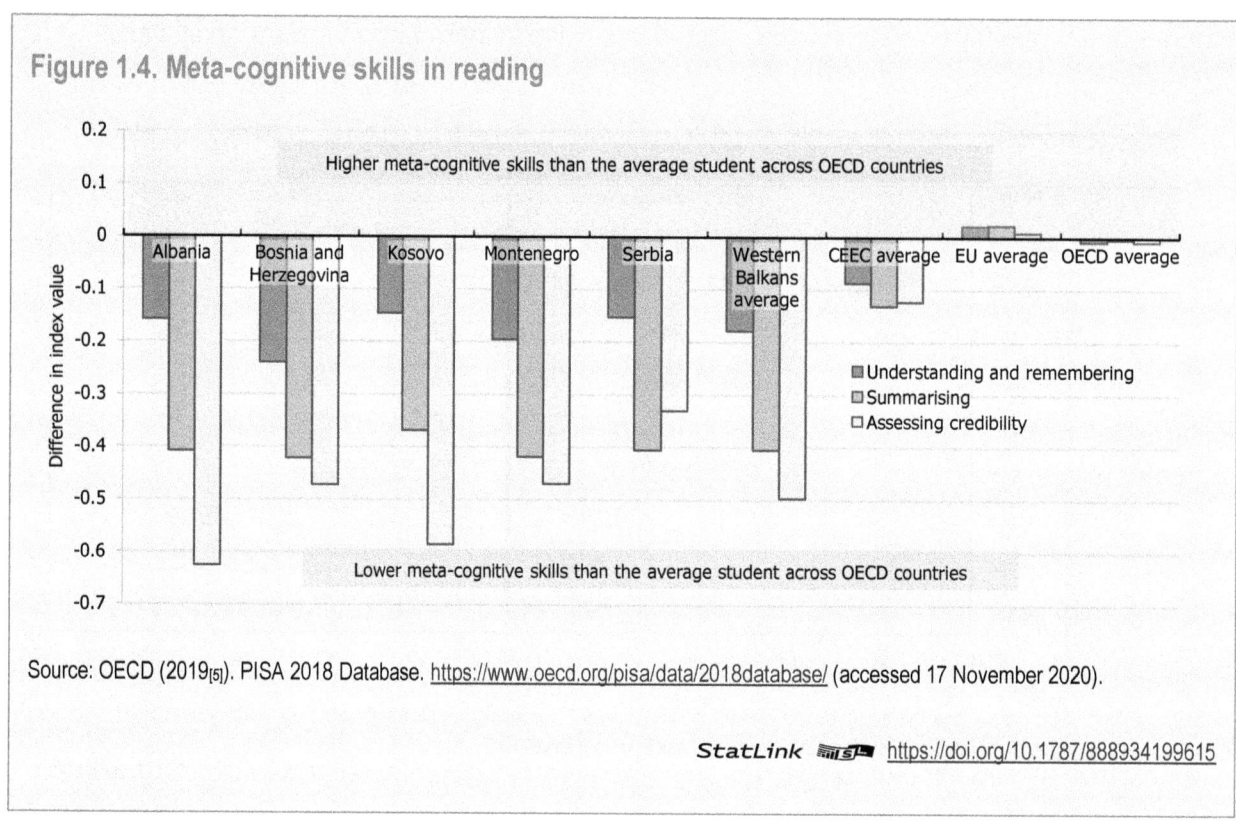

Figure 1.4. Meta-cognitive skills in reading

Source: OECD (2019[5]). PISA 2018 Database. https://www.oecd.org/pisa/data/2018database/ (accessed 17 November 2020).

StatLink https://doi.org/10.1787/888934199615

Performance and equity

In addition to overall performance, PISA measures the outcomes of different student groups within an education system. This type of disaggregation helps policy makers understand if all students are achieving similar outcomes, or if some students are performing very well while others are falling behind. This paper concentrates primarily on equity according to students' socio-economic status and their educational track and, when relevant, language and gender, which are important educational issues in the region.

Socio-economic status

Internationally, socio-economically advantaged students tend to perform better than disadvantaged students in all PISA-participating countries and economies, and education systems in the Western Balkans are no exception (Figure 1.5). Gaps between socio-economically advantaged and disadvantaged students range from 40 score points in Kosovo to 80 score points in North Macedonia. These gaps are, in general, narrower than those of countries with similar overall performance[5]. Such results suggest that students' socio-economic status may not be as strong a determinant of their outcomes compared to international benchmarks. However, it is still an important factor, and other chapters of this paper will discuss the extent to which education policy is helping to address such inequalities.

Figure 1.5. Socio-economic status and student performance

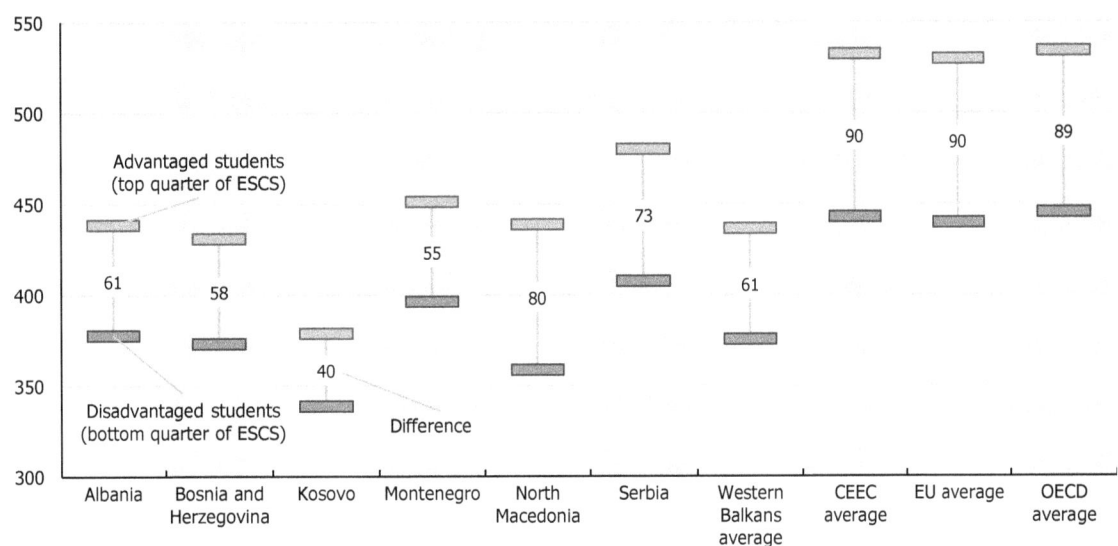

Note: All differences are statistically significant.
Source: OECD (2019[5]). PISA 2018 Database. https://www.oecd.org/pisa/data/2018database/ (accessed 17 November 2020), Tables I.B1.2.3.

StatLink https://doi.org/10.1787/888934199634

Geographic location

PISA 2018 results showed that students enrolled in schools in urban areas generally outperform those enrolled in rural schools, though the gap disappeared once the socio-economic status of students and schools was accounted for (OECD, 2019[11]). The only education systems in the Western Balkans with enough 15-year-old students enrolled in rural schools to be analysed — Albania, Bosnia and Herzegovina[6] and Kosovo — show considerable rural-urban gaps in reading performance (OECD, 2019[12]). In these three education systems, students in urban schools outperformed those in rural schools by about 50 score points, similar to the gap observed across OECD countries. After controlling for students' socio-economic status, gaps ranged from 34 to 36 and were all statistically significant.

Educational tracks

Internationally and in the Western Balkans, reading performance also varies according to education tracks. On average across the region, students enrolled in general education programmes scored 435 points in reading, whereas those enrolled in vocational programmes scored 382 points. The largest gap was in Serbia (85 score points) and the narrowest was in Albania (25 score points). Similar results are observed when considering the share of low-achieving students, or those who score at or below Level 2. Across the Western Balkans, about 65% of students enrolled in a vocational programme were classified as low achieving, compared to only 34% of students attending a general education programme (Figure 1.6).

Figure 1.6. Low-achieving students and educational programmes

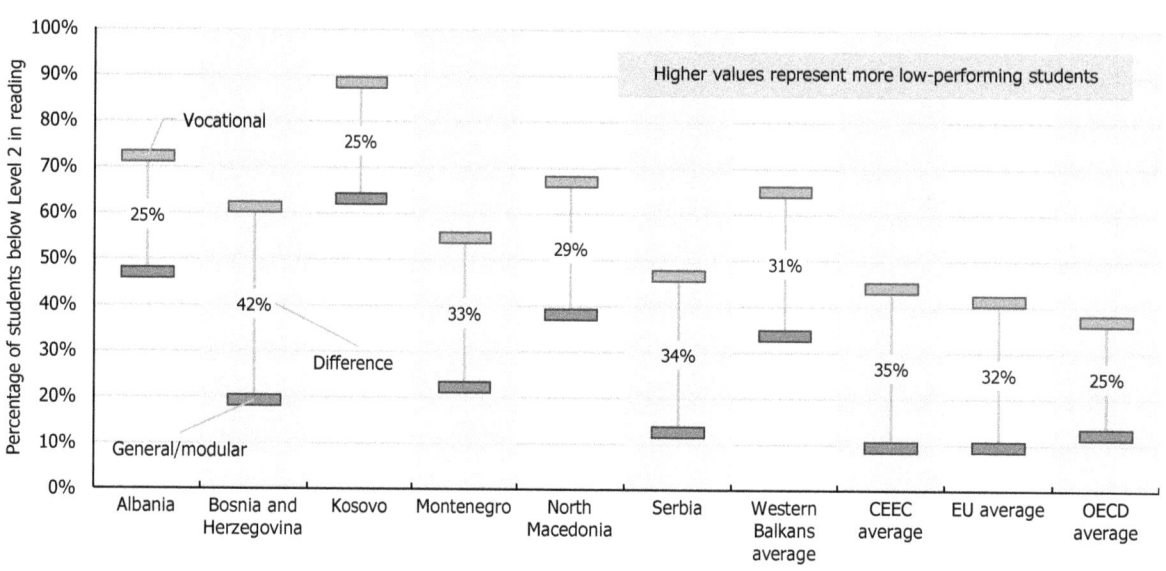

Note: All differences are statistically significant.
Source: OECD (2019[5]). PISA 2018 Database. https://www.oecd.org/pisa/data/2018database/ (accessed 17 November 2020).

StatLink https://doi.org/10.1787/888934199653

Gender

PISA results consistently show that girls tend to outperform boys by about 30 points in reading. In mathematics, boys out perform girls by roughly five points, and differences in science are inconclusive. In the Western Balkans, girls outperform boys in reading and science (differences in mathematics are inconclusive), but the gaps are decreasing over time (in general, both genders are showing performance increases) (OECD, 2019[11]). However, there is considerable variation between systems. North Macedonia, for instance, had a gender gap in reading of 51 score points, which was one of the largest in PISA. In North Macedonia, gender alone explains roughly 7% of the variation in student performance, compared to only 2% across OECD countries. This gap has persisted since North Macedonia joined PISA in 2000 (Figure 1.7).

Figure 1.7. Differences in reading performance by gender over time

Results are shown as the difference between girls and boys (girls minus boys)

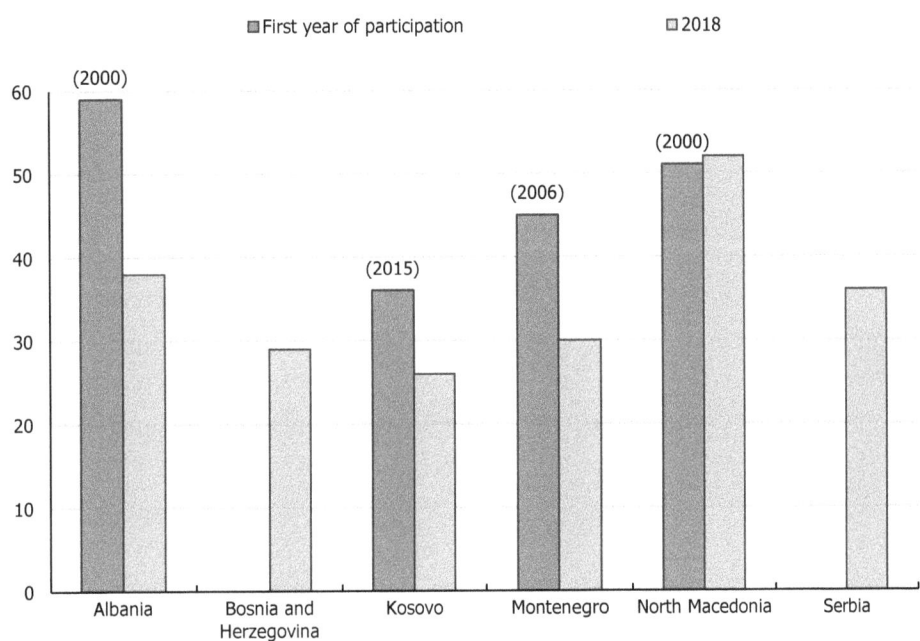

Note: Serbia participated in 2006 and 2009 but did not meet reporting standards that allowed for disaggregation by gender. Bosnia and Herzegovina participated for the first time in 2018.
Source: OECD (2019[5]). PISA 2018 Database. https://www.oecd.org/pisa/data/2018database/ (accessed 17 November 2020). Tables II.B1.7.29, Table II.B1.7.30.

StatLink https://doi.org/10.1787/888934038704

The relatively lower overall performance of the region and persistent gender performance gap means that boys in the Western Balkans are at significant risk of not mastering the basic skills that are important for individual and societal development. In PISA 2018, over 61% of boys in the region scored below Level 2 in reading, compared to 45% of girls. These results point to the need for more attention to how boys are taught and assessed, as well as to elements in school and wider society that undermine boys' engagement in education and could lead to poor behaviour, truancy and absenteeism.

It should also be noted that in Kosovo and Montenegro, boys are more socio-economically advantaged to statistically significant degrees. These discrepancies could suggest a participation bias with respect to student populations that enrol in (or drop out from) secondary education. Furthermore, since socio-economically advantaged students tend to score higher in PISA, in these systems the gap between girls and boys are greater after socio-economic status is taken into consideration.

Linguistic groups

Within the Western Balkans, education systems with large populations of different ethnic groups demonstrate different levels of performance between the populations (represented by their languages of instruction). In Bosnia and Herzegovina, the performance of students in the three languages of instruction are not statistically significantly different from each other. In North Macedonia and Montenegro, however, students taught in Albanian perform significantly lower than students taught in Macedonian and Montenegrin, respectively. In fact, no student who took the test in Albanian was considered a high achiever (achieving Level 5 or above) in either system. After controlling for students' socio-economic status, the gap in Macedonia was 48 and the gap in Montenegro was 66 and both were statistically significant. Gaps in Bosnia and Herzegovina were less than three (Croatian and Serbian relative to Bosnian) and not statistically significant. These results suggest that it is not enough to provide access to education in different languages of instruction, but that teachers who teach in different languages and their schools need to receive adequate support to ensure that their students are educated effectively (Figure 1.8).

Figure 1.8. Performance in reading by language of instruction

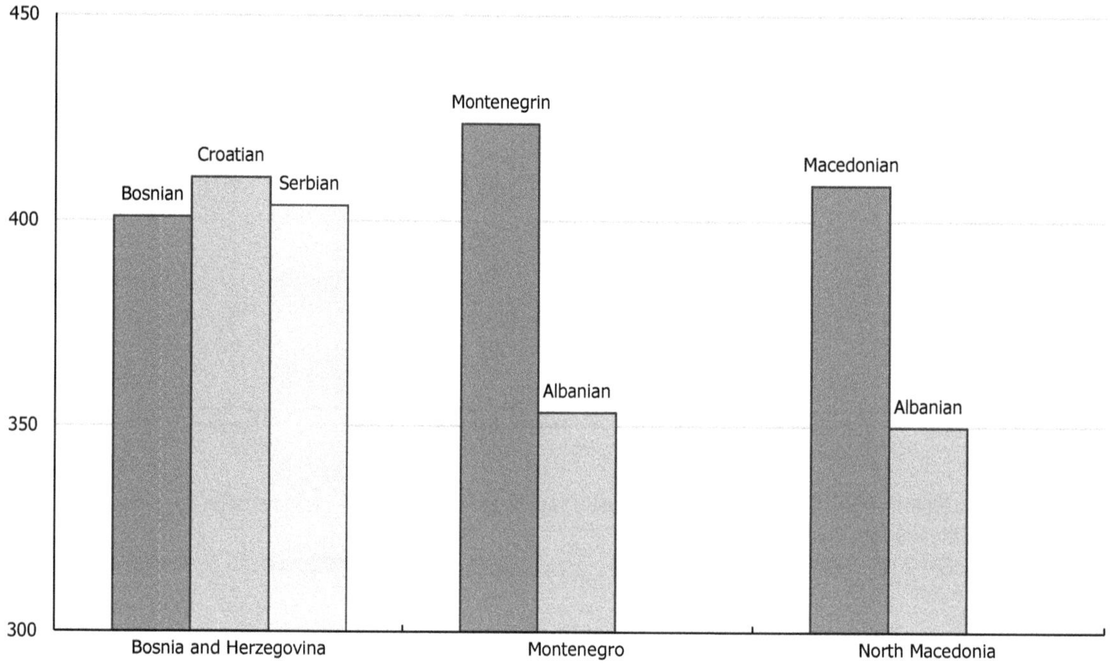

Source: OECD (2019[5]). PISA 2018 Database. https://www.oecd.org/pisa/data/2018database/ (accessed 17 November 2020).

StatLink https://doi.org/10.1787/888934199672

References

Echazarra, A. and T. Radinger (2019), "Learning in rural schools: Insights from PISA, TALIS and the literature", *OECD Education Working Papers*, No. 196, OECD Publishing, Paris, https://dx.doi.org/10.1787/8b1a5cb9-en. [6]

European CommissionEACEA/Eurydice (2018), *Compulsory Education in Europe – 2018/19*, Publications Office of the European Union, Luxembourg, http://dx.doi.org/10.2797/20126. [7]

European Union (2019), *The Western Balkans*, https://www.europarl.europa.eu/factsheets/en/sheet/168/the-western-balkans (accessed on 9 September 2020). [13]

Maghnouj, S. et al. (2020), *OECD Reviews of Evaluation and Assessment in Education: Albania*, OECD Reviews of Evaluation and Assessment in Education, OECD Publishing, Paris, https://dx.doi.org/10.1787/d267dc93-en. [3]

Maghnouj, S. et al. (2019), *OECD Reviews of Evaluation and Assessment in Education: Serbia*, OECD Reviews of Evaluation and Assessment in Education, OECD Publishing, Paris, https://dx.doi.org/10.1787/225350d9-en. [2]

OECD (2019), *OECD Reviews of Evaluation and Assessment in Education: North Macedonia*, OECD Reviews of Evaluation and Assessment in Education, OECD Publishing, Paris, https://dx.doi.org/10.1787/079fe34c-en. [1]

OECD (2019), *PISA*, OECD Publishing, Paris, https://dx.doi.org/101787/b25efab8-en. [10]

OECD (2019), *PISA 2018 Database*, https://www.oecd.org/pisa/data/2018database/ (accessed on 17 November 2020). [5]

OECD (2019), *PISA 2018 Results (Volume I): What Students Know and Can Do*, OECD Publishing, Paris. [9]

OECD (2019), *PISA 2018 Results (Volume II): Where All Students Can Succeed*, PISA, OECD Publishing, Paris, https://dx.doi.org/10.1787/b5fd1b8f-en. [11]

OECD (2019), *PISA 2018 Results (Volume III): What School Life Means for Students' Lives*, PISA, OECD Publishing, Paris, https://dx.doi.org/10.1787/acd78851-en. [12]

OECD (2019), *PISA Assessment and Analytical Framework*. [14]

OECD (2010), *Learning for Jobs*, OECD Reviews of Vocational Education and Training, OECD Publishing, Paris, https://dx.doi.org/10.1787/9789264087460-en. [8]

OECD (n.d.), , https://dx.doi.org/10.1787/b25efab8-en. [15]

The World Bank (n.d.), *GDP per capita (current US$) | Data*, https://data.worldbank.org/indicator/NY.GDP.PCAP.CD?locations=XK-AL-ME-MK-RS&view=chart (accessed on 1 February 2019). [4]

Notes

[1] The European Union defines the Western Balkans as Albania, Bosnia and Herzegovina, Kosovo*, Montenegro, the Republic of North Macedonia and Serbia (European Union, 2019[13]).

*All references to Kosovo, whether the territory, institutions or population, in this text are without prejudice to positions on status and shall be understood in full compliance with the United Nations Security Council Resolution 1244/99 and the Advisory Opinion of the International Court of Justice on Kosovo's declaration of independence.

[2] The OECD considers CEEC to be composed of Albania, Bulgaria, Croatia, the Czech Republic, Estonia, Hungary, Latvia, Lithuania, Poland, Romania, the Slovak Republic and Slovenia. For this paper, results that represent the CEEC average are calculated without data from Albania to avoid overlap with results that represent the Western Balkans average.

[3] According to the PISA student questionnaire, a student with an immigrant background is defined as having been born in a different country than where he/she currently resides, or having at least one parent who was born in a different country than where the student resides.

[4] Most of this paper will discuss PISA results in reading as reading was the domain that received the most focus in PISA 2018.

[5] Countries with similar overall performance are used as a comparison point because there is a relationship between the size of performance gaps and the overall range of performance of a country.

[6] Bosnia and Herzegovina's education system largely operates as 12 separate systems, but these were not oversampled representatively. Therefore, results for Bosnia and Herzegovina are presented as one system.

2 Delivering effective and equitable schooling

Introduction

Schools are at the heart of education systems. How they deliver teaching and learning opportunities can contribute to the achievement of not only educational goals, but also broader development goals, such as participatory citizenship, social cohesion and economic competitiveness. Western Balkan economies have enacted important school-level policies to improve the excellence and equity of schooling. These efforts include the introduction of modern, competence-based curricula, the development of comprehensive school evaluation systems, and a shift towards more needs-based resourcing of schools.

Nevertheless, data from PISA and OECD-UNICEF country reviews suggest that several challenges remain in terms of school effectiveness. An important overarching issue is that schooling in the region, in addition to demonstrating relatively lower performance, is not equitable. At the upper-secondary level, students are rigidly tracked and selection into these tracks reflects – and risks exacerbating – inequities at lower educational levels. These inequities develop partly because overall spending in the education sector is low and inefficient compared to international benchmarks, and because schools with more disadvantaged students often receive fewer resources. Against this backdrop, rapid urbanisation is shrinking schools in rural areas creating pressures for more efficient and equitable resource allocation.

This chapter uses PISA data to analyse how schooling in the Western Balkans is both similar to and different from international benchmarks. It focuses strongly on examining how different levels of school inputs, from their student intake to their infrastructure, might be leading to different types of outcomes. Based on these findings, it suggests potential reforms that might help education systems in the region improve learning for all students.

Student tracking

Similar to many OECD countries, Western Balkan education systems track students into general and vocational programmes at the upper-secondary level. However, what distinguishes student tracking in the Western Balkans is the size of vocational sectors and the lack of permeability between educational tracks. As a student's track strongly affects his/her academic and professional opportunities, policy makers must carefully consider how to place students into different tracks and how to help students along their different trajectories. Sorting mechanisms must be reliable and equitable and all students, regardless of what educational track they enter, should be supported to succeed in future learning, work and life.

Data from PISA

Placement into upper-secondary tracks is highly selective

Compared to international benchmarks, Western Balkan systems are much more academically selective when allocating students into educational tracks. For example, some 45% of upper-secondary students from OECD countries attend a school where admission is contingent upon academic performance, compared to 69% of students in the Western Balkans (Table 2.1). In fact, at the upper-secondary level, Western Balkan education systems are some of the most academically selective in the world (Figure 2.1), which increases the need for selection mechanisms to be fair and reliable.

Table 2.1. Criteria for admission into upper-secondary schools

Percentage of students in schools whose principal reported the following:

	Student's record of academic performance is always considered for school admission		Residence in a particular area is always considered for school admission	
	Lower-secondary education	Upper-secondary education	Lower-secondary education	Upper-secondary education
Albania	52	62	43	46
Bosnia and Herzegovina	23	73	69	7
Kosovo	51	92	35	7
Montenegro	49	50	45	17
North Macedonia	c	49	c	6
Serbia	c	85	c	4
Western Balkans average	44	69	48	15
CEEC average	15	74	57	13
EU average	19	51	54	29
OECD average	20	45	50	32

Note: Darker tones indicate greater academic selectivity of the school system.
Student's record of academic performance is always considered for school admission:
☐ Less than 20
☐ 20 to 40
▨ 40 to 60
■ Greater than 60
Residence in a particular area is always considered for school admission:
☐ Greater than 60
☐ 40 to 60
▨ 20 to 40
■ Less than 20
Source: OECD (2019[1]). PISA 2018 Database. https://www.oecd.org/pisa/data/2018database/ (accessed 17 November 2020).

StatLink ᔖᲘᲑᲚ https://doi.org/10.1787/888934199691

Figure 2.1. Academic selectivity into upper secondary schools in international education systems

Only students in upper-secondary school

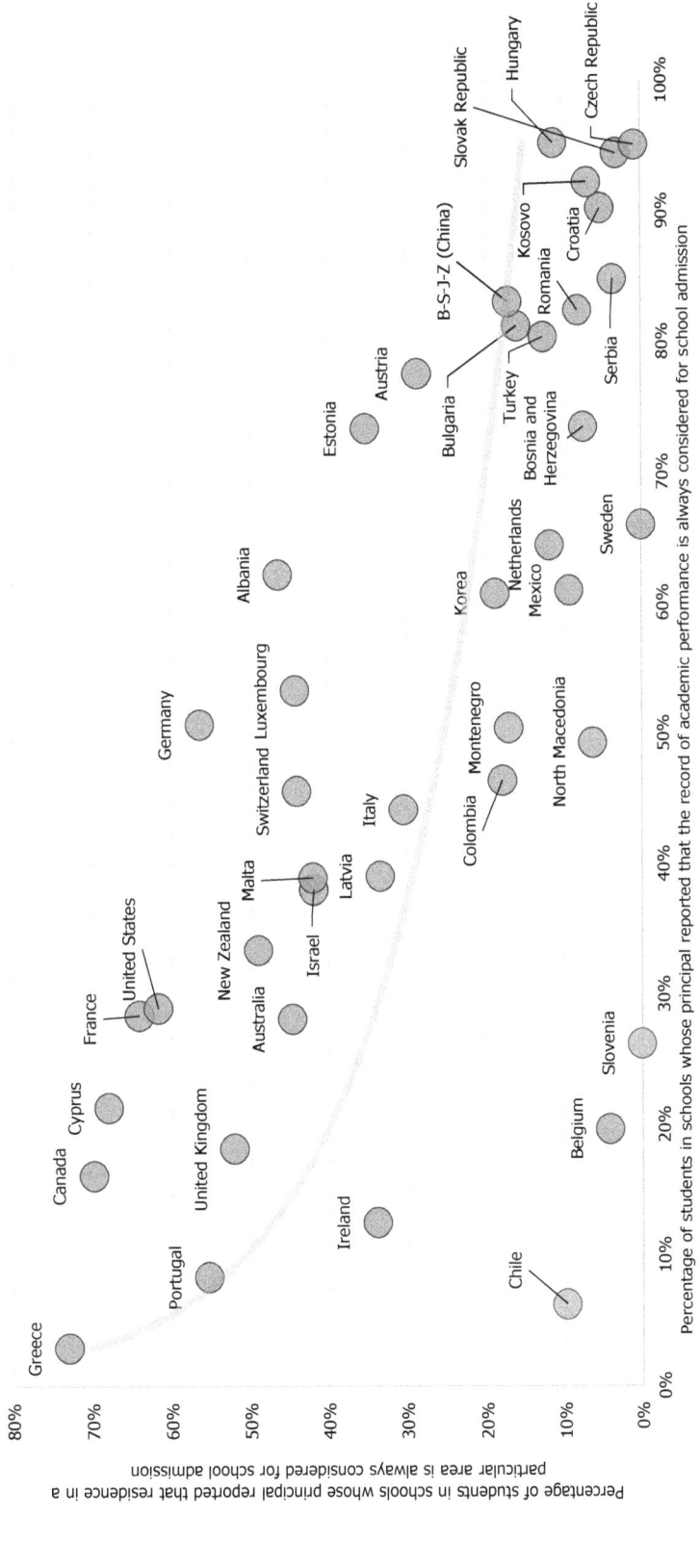

Source: OECD (2019[1]), PISA 2018 Database, https://www.oecd.org/pisa/data/2018database/ (accessed 17 November 2020).

StatLink https://doi.org/10.1787/888934199710

Selection mechanisms in the Western Balkans are not reliable

For highly selective education systems to be equitable, the determinations of student ability that place them into tracks must be valid and reliable. However, data from PISA suggest that assessments of student ability in the Western Balkans might not be accurate and might be largely reflecting student demographics (e.g. their gender and socio-economic background) instead of student capability. This disconnect can then impact the equity of tracking decisions.

For example, on average across Western Balkan systems, students who attend vocational programmes are over twice as likely to be male and almost three times as likely to be socio-economically disadvantaged than students in general education programmes (Figure 2.2). While these results are consistent with the OECD average, there are considerable differences at the system level. In Serbia, socio-economically disadvantaged students are more than five times as likely to attend a vocational upper-secondary school. In Albania, on the other hand, advantaged and disadvantaged students are equally likely to attend vocational upper-secondary school.

Figure 2.2. Increased likelihood of attending a vocational programme according to gender and socio-economic status

Only students in upper-secondary school

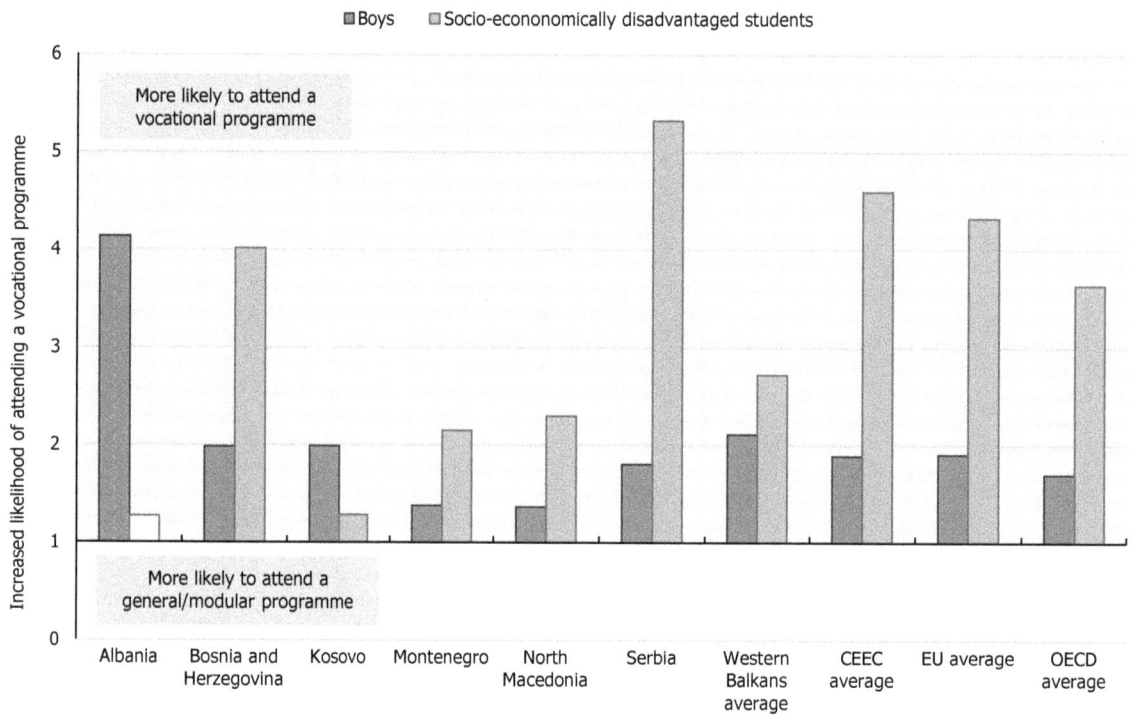

Notes: Values that are statistically significant are shaded.
Results based on logistic regression models; one for each variable.
Reference categories are girls and socio-economically non-disadvantaged students.
Source: OECD (2019[1]). PISA 2018 Database. https://www.oecd.org/pisa/data/2018database/ (accessed 17 November 2020).

StatLink https://doi.org/10.1787/888934199729

These findings help explain some of the disparities in learning outcomes between tracks that were illustrated in Chapter 1. Since boys and disadvantaged students are also more likely to attend vocational programmes, performance differences between educational tracks expectedly decrease after accounting for these variables (Figure 2.3). The extent to which these variables account for performance differences can indicate how much tracking decisions reflect differences in student ability or student background. In the Western Balkans, this measure differs considerably across systems, suggesting that some tracking mechanisms might be strongly reflecting student background. In Serbia, for example, the average performance difference between tracks drops 64 score points after accounting for gender and socio-economic status, a considerably larger change than the average change across the OECD (40 score points). In North Macedonia, accounting for these variables shrinks performance differences between general and vocational tracks to 17 points, the lowest performance gap in the region and considerably lower than the OECD, EU and CEEC averages.

Figure 2.3. Performance differences between general education and vocational students

Difference in score points in reading before and after controlling for gender and socio-economic status, only students in upper-secondary school

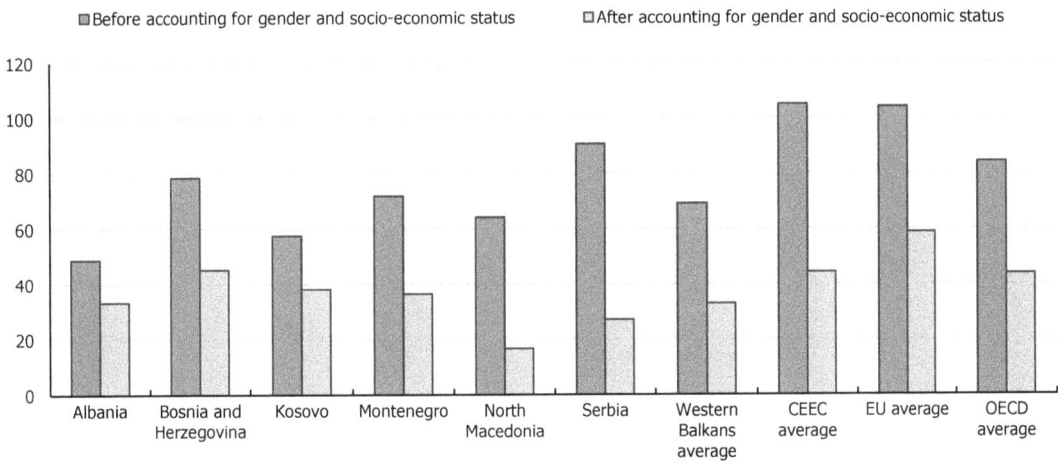

Notes: All differences are statistically significant. Results based on linear regression analyses.
Source: OECD (2019[1]). PISA 2018 Database. https://www.oecd.org/pisa/data/2018database/ (accessed 17 November 2020).

StatLink https://doi.org/10.1787/888934199748

Many vocational students do not master core cognitive competences

Education systems have a responsibility to ensure that all students, regardless of their educational track, receive quality instruction. Results from PISA indicate that many Western Balkan systems are struggling to equip a large share of students, especially those in vocational programmes, with basic literacy and numeracy skills (see Chapter 1). This disparity is partly because vocational students may face equity challenges in lower level schooling that contribute to weaker foundational skills. However, if vocational programmes do not effectively help students strengthen these important skills, disparities in learning outcomes can actually widen after students are tracked.

Using PISA data, OECD analysts examined the difference in performance between students in different grades in upper-secondary education in vocational programmes compared to general education programmes (i.e. the change observed in one year of schooling in both programmes). In EU countries for which data are available, such as Italy and Hungary, the increase in achievement across grades is actually greater in vocational tracks, revealing the potential of vocational programmes to address critical learning gaps. In Western Balkan systems with available data, however, students in vocational programmes demonstrate less increased achievement across grades compared to students in general education tracks (Figure 2.4). This widening learning gap is especially problematic in the Western Balkans since students cannot switch programmes or take courses from other tracks once they are selected into their upper-secondary pathways. Unless vocational programmes can effectively develop the competences that students need to be economically competitive, students might not take vocational education seriously, which could further widen learning disparities between tracks and contribute to social and economic issues (Box 2.1).

Figure 2.4. Difference in student performance between students in different grades in general education and vocational programmes

Difference in score points in reading between upper-secondary students in consecutive grades (higher grade students minus lower grade students), after accounting for socio-economic status and gender

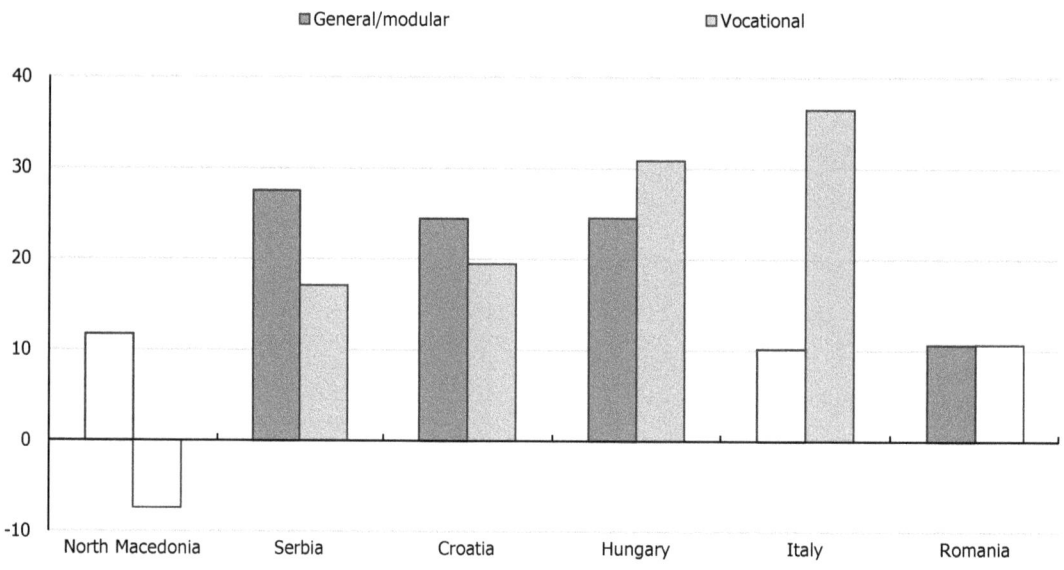

Notes: Values that are not statistically insignificant are not shaded.
Only North Macedonia and Serbia are shown because other Western Balkan economies do not have large enough student samples in consecutive grades at the upper-secondary level.
The two consecutive grade levels with the most students were chosen for analysis. In each country, these grade levels were 9 and 10.
Comparison countries are those from the EU who track at the upper-secondary level and have sufficient student sample sizes in consecutive grades at the upper-secondary level.
Source: OECD (2019[11]). PISA 2018 Database. https://www.oecd.org/pisa/data/2018database/ (accessed 17 November 2020).

StatLink https://doi.org/10.1787/888934199767

Box 2.1. Student behaviour in general education and vocational programmes

PISA 2018 asked students questions about their behaviour in school. Answers to these questions were used to create an index of disciplinary climate and an index of sense of belonging at school. These indices are calibrated such that the OECD average is zero, and a value of one represents one standard deviation away from the OECD average. Like international benchmarks, students in the Western

Balkans who are enrolled in general education programmes believe their classmates demonstrate better discipline and feel a greater sense of belonging than students enrolled in vocational programmes, who are also more likely to be truant (Figure 2.5).

Figure 2.5. Student behaviour in general education and vocational programmes

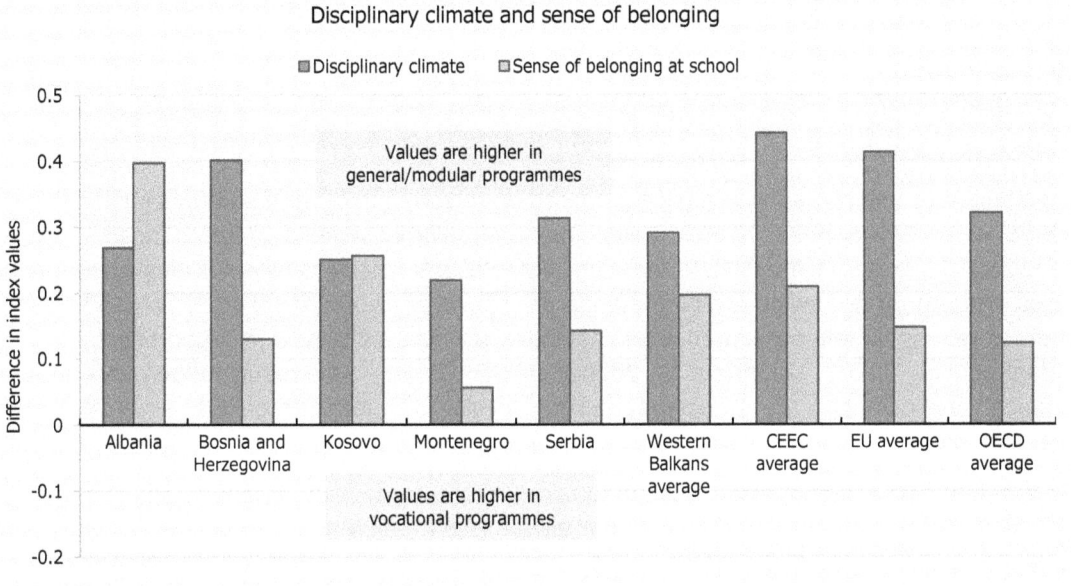

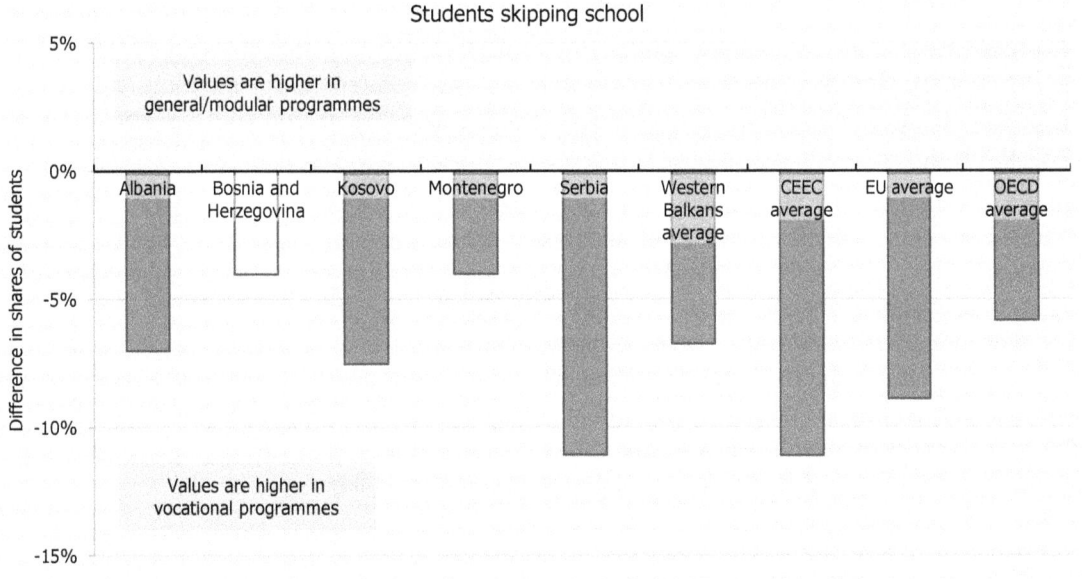

Note: Values that are not statistically insignificant are not shaded.
Source: OECD (2019[1]). PISA 2018 Database. https://www.oecd.org/pisa/data/2018database/ (accessed 17 November 2020).

StatLink https://doi.org/10.1787/888934199786

> Several factors might explain these findings. One is that vocational students, who are more likely to have lower performance and be boys, are also more likely to demonstrate associated behaviours, such as being less disciplined and skipping school. Another is that vocational students recognise that they have been placed in what is perceived to be a "lesser" track and thus take their schooling less seriously. These results are troubling because they could lead to disengagement, dropout and unemployment, especially among boys, which OECD-UNICEF reviews have noted are issues in the region.

Policy implications

Improving student assessment can make tracking decisions more equitable

Tracking students equitably requires having a shared understanding of what students should know and be able to do at a certain point in their education, and reliably assessing them against that shared understanding. To better communicate learning expectations, many Western Balkan economies have introduced modern, system-wide learning standards. However, there is generally limited understanding about how to assess student performance against these standards and how to support students to achieve them (Maghnouj, S., 2020[2]; Maghnouj, S., 2020[3]; OECD, 2019[4]). As a result, judgements about student performance (and potential) are sometimes subject to bias and inconsistencies, which can compound inequities that often start in earlier years of schooling and contribute to inequitable tracking outcomes.

Several Western Balkan economies have undertaken efforts to develop teachers' assessment capacity. North Macedonia, for example, introduced a Formative Assessment Manual. In Serbia, teachers administer mandatory diagnostic tests at the beginning of each school year to develop a baseline for evaluating individual student progress (OECD, 2019[4]; Maghnouj, S., 2020[3]). These types of formative assessments, or assessments *for* learning, can help teachers identify more reliably and support struggling students (OECD, 2013[5]). Another way that many education systems, including a growing number in the Western Balkans, support teachers' assessment literacy is through the use of national assessments. These are centrally developed, standardised tests that do not have consequences for students but can serve as models for teachers to develop their own standards-based assessments and help teachers moderate their classroom grading.

To improve the fairness of the tracking decision itself, most Western Balkan economies administer examinations to inform selection into upper-secondary schools. Unlike national assessments, exams do carry consequences for students but, if reliable, can provide a less subjective, external measure of student learning so tracking decisions are not determined solely by teacher judgements. North Macedonia, which has very narrow performance gaps between general education and vocational students when student background is accounted for (and large disparities when background is unaccounted for) is the only system in the region with neither a national assessment nor a lower-secondary examination (Table 2.2). This example highlights the risk that tracking decisions made solely based on teacher judgement without external moderation might reflect student background more than ability.

Table 2.2. External assessments and examinations in the Western Balkans

Grades when national assessments and examinations are administered

	National assessment (grades)	National examination (levels after which the examination is administered)	
		Lower-secondary	Upper-secondary
Albania	5	X	X
Bosnia and Herzegovina	Varies	Varies	Varies
Kosovo		X	X
Montenegro		X	X
North Macedonia	Under development	-	X
Serbia	Under development	X	X

Notes: Serbia's current examination at the end of upper-secondary education is school-based, meaning it is developed, administered and marked in each school and is thus not standardised across the system. A centralised examination is planned to be introduced in 2020.
Bosnia and Herzegovina's policies differ according to internal education systems.

While vocational curricula preparation should focus on occupational skills, research shows that core academic skills, such as functional literacy and numeracy, are also important for students to succeed in the workplace and adjust to accelerated changes in the world of work. Successful vocational programmes, therefore, develop students' core cognitive skills alongside occupational skills. Findings from OECD-UNICEF policy reviews in the Western Balkans, however, indicate that vocational curricula might focus too much on foundational skills from a theoretical perspective as opposed to a practical one (Maghnouj, S., 2020[3]; OECD, 2019[4]). Data from PISA further highlight the considerable need for vocational programmes to help students develop fundamental competences, especially in the Western Balkans where large shares of students have not achieved basic literacy and numeracy skills by age 15.

Ensuring that all upper-secondary students, including those in vocational tracks, develop foundational skills requires a range of policy measures that motivate students to learn, from introducing flexibility between pathways to providing career guidance and access to tertiary education (OECD, 2010[6]). Another policy area that requires particular attention is examinations, which can help drive teaching and learning, signal skills to employers through certification and create diverse opportunities so students do not perceive vocational education to be a "dead end" (Figure 2.6) (OECD, 2013[5]).

Most Western Balkan economies already have well-established upper-secondary exams, commonly known as maturas, which include a set of mandatory subjects that are taken by both general education and vocational students (Table 2.2). By allowing all students to enter tertiary education, maturas help raise the value of vocational programmes. More can be done, however, especially regarding recognising students' vocational abilities in addition to their academic ones (Box 2.2).

Box 2.2. Strengthening the value of vocational education

Internationally, students and parents sometimes consider vocational education to be a less prestigious track, which can discourage vocational students from taking their schooling seriously and undermine national economic goals. PISA 2018 findings suggest this might be an issue in the Western Balkans, as almost half of vocational students in the region expect to complete a four year bachelor's degree (Figure 2.6). On one hand, this finding reflects a positive feature of Western Balkan education systems, that vocational students are not deterred from pursuing academic tertiary studies. However, it may also reflect a belief that vocational programmes do not adequately prepare students to secure a good job.

Making vocational education valuable is a challenge in many countries. One way of enhancing the attractiveness and rigour of vocational education is conferring a certification that is equivalent to students from general education programmes, and which allows for entry into university. Also important is ensuring that students are certified for their vocational skills, which would give them a competitive advantage compared to individuals who do not hold such a certification. In Germany and Switzerland, this type of external recognition is conferred through students' examination results (and validated by chambers of industry) in specific vocational subjects.

Currently, almost all vocational and general education students in the Western Balkans receive the same upper-secondary certification. However, there is no externally validated certification of specific vocational competences, which might make it more challenging for vocational students to find meaningful employment and make the vocational track seem less attractive.

Figure 2.6. Differences in expectations between students who attend general education and vocational programmes

Percentage of upper-secondary students who expect to complete a university degree

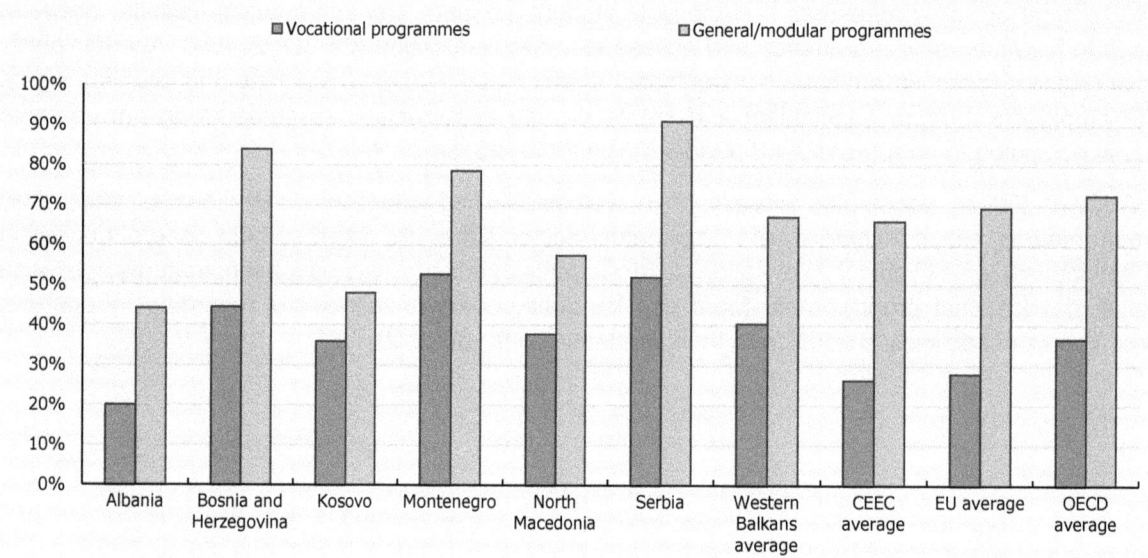

Notes: A university degree includes a Bachelor's, Master's or Doctoral degree (ISCED 5A and 6).
All differences are statistically significant.
Source: OECD (2019[1]). PISA 2018 Database. https://www.oecd.org/pisa/data/2018database/ (accessed 17 November 2020).

StatLink https://doi.org/10.1787/888934199805

School resourcing

On average across the Western Balkans, education spending as a percentage of gross domestic product (GDP) is much smaller than that of OECD and EU countries (Table 2.3). As a result, education systems in the region face a range of resource concerns from school buildings in need of major repairs (maintenance) to deficient technological infrastructure that impedes computer-based assessment (OECD, 2019[4]; World Bank, 2019[7]). Within this context, it is even more important for education systems to allocate resources in ways that best support high quality teaching and learning for all students.

Table 2.3. Education system funding

Economy	Education funding (all levels) as percentage of GDP (year)
Albania	4.0 (2016)
Bosnia and Herzegovina	Data not available
Kosovo	4.7 (2014)
Montenegro	Around 4.0% (2017)
North Macedonia	3.7 (2016)
Serbia	4.0 (2015)
CEEC average	4.5% (2016)
EU average	5.0% (2016)
OECD average	5.4 (2016)

Sources: Kosovo Ministry of Education (2016[8]). Kosovo Education Strategic Plan 2017-2021. http://www.kryeministri-ks.net/repository/docs/KOSOVO_EDUCATION_STRATEGIC_PLAN.pdf (accessed 20 March 2020).
International Monetary Fund (2017[9]). Montenegro: Selected Issues. https://www.imf.org/~/media/Files/Publications/CR/2017/cr17277.ashx (accessed 17 November 2020).
UNESCO-UIS (n.d.[10]). Government expenditure on education as a percentage of GDP. http://data.uis.unesco.org/# (accessed 20 March 2020).

Data from PISA

Overall educational resourcing is lower in the Western Balkans

PISA 2018 asks education systems to provide system-level data about educational expenditure. On average across the four Western Balkan economies for which data were available, spending on the education of a single student through age 15 was roughly 26 000 USD, considerably less than the OECD average of around 89 000 per student.

Figure 2.7 shows the relationship between cumulative per student spending through age 15 vis-à-vis mean performance on the PISA reading test. The picture for the Western Balkans is mixed. Serbia and Montenegro perform higher than would be expected, while Bosnia and Herzegovina and North Macedonia perform lower than would be expected given their level of spending. These findings suggest that while the overall level of funding of an education system matters, the design of its education policies (i.e. the efficiency of spending) can also affect learning outcomes.

Figure 2.7. Cumulative spending through age 15 and relationship with performance

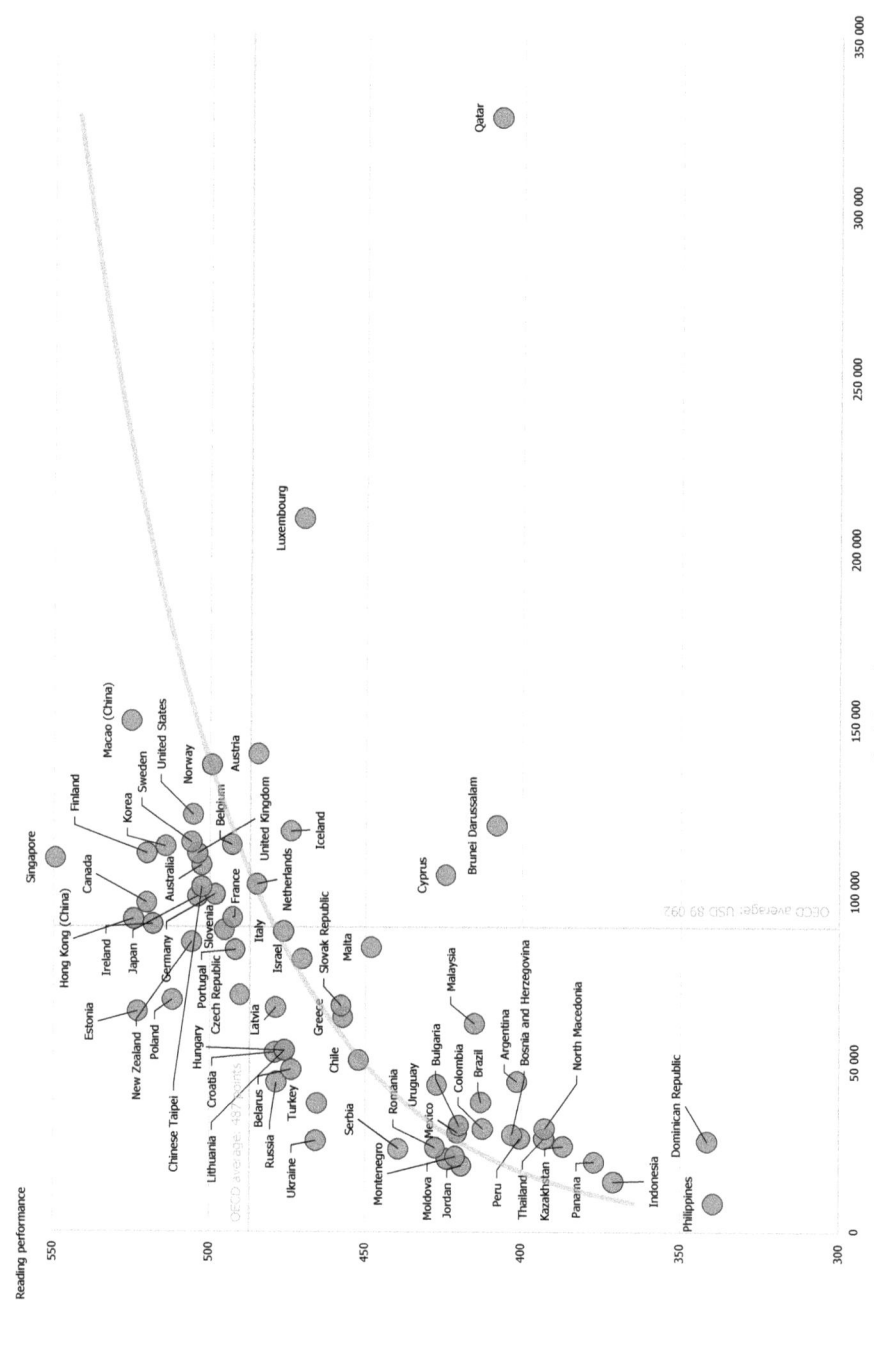

Source: OECD (2019[1]). PISA 2018 Database: https://www.oecd.org/pisa/data/2018database/ (accessed 17 November 2020). Tables I.B1.4 and B3.1.1.

To better understand school resourcing, PISA 2018 asked school principals to indicate whether a shortage or inadequacy of key educational resources hindered instruction at their schools. These key resources are defined here as:

- physical infrastructure (e.g. school buildings, heating and cooling systems, and instructional space)
- educational materials (e.g. textbooks, laboratory equipment, instructional material and computers)
- human resources (i.e. teachers and teaching assistants).

Table 2.4 shows how principals in the Western Balkans responded to questions about these resources compared to principals from other education systems. On average, principals from the Western Balkans are slightly more likely to report that inadequate material resources (defined by PISA as both educational materials and physical infrastructure) hinders instruction at their schools. Principals from Bosnia and Herzegovina and Kosovo are considerably more likely to report issues with material resources.

In terms of human resources, there is very little variation across Western Balkan economies. This finding is in line with other PISA data showing that distributions of certified teachers and those with master's degrees (proxies for teacher quality) in the Western Balkans are similar across schools, regardless of differences in curricula programmes or student populations. While these results suggest that the allocation of educational staff is not a major concern for the region at the systems level, there are noticeable disparities in instructional practices among different types of schools, highlighting a need for policies to go beyond focusing on teacher certification and qualification levels to more closely examine differences in teaching practices across schools. Chapter 3 studies these issues in greater detail.

Table 2.4. Principals' perceptions of key educational resources

Percentage of students in schools whose principal reported that the school's capacity to provide instruction was hindered a lot by:

	Material resources			
	A lack of educational material	Inadequate or poor quality educational material	A lack of physical infrastructure	Inadequate or poor quality physical infrastructure
Albania	8	5	7	6
Bosnia and Herzegovina	18	16	13	13
Kosovo	33	22	18	15
Montenegro	5	3	5	7
North Macedonia	16	7	8	8
Serbia	5	3	6	8
Western Balkans average	14	9	9	10
CEEC average	4	4	9	9
EU average	4	4	9	10
OECD average	5	4	9	9

	Human resources			
	A lack of teaching staff	Inadequate or poorly qualified teaching staff	A lack of assisting staff	Inadequate or poorly qualified assisting staff
Albania	1	1	3	2
Bosnia and Herzegovina	0	0	2	0
Kosovo	2	3	7	3
Montenegro	0	0	2	0
North Macedonia	1	1	5	0
Serbia	0	0	4	0
Western Balkans average	1	1	4	1
CEEC average	3	1	6	1
EU average	4	1	9	3
OECD average	4	1	8	3

Note: Darker tones indicate greater reported lack of resources.
☐ Less than 5
☐ 5 to 10
☐ 10 to 15
☐ 15 to 20
■ Greater than 20
Source: OECD (2019[1]). PISA 2018 Database. https://www.oecd.org/pisa/data/2018database/ (accessed 17 November 2020).

StatLink https://doi.org/10.1787/888934199824

Educational resourcing in the Western Balkans is inequitable

In addition to the overall level of resource provision, it is important to consider whether resources are going to where they are most needed. Across OECD countries, material resources are not allocated equitably across schools. In general, advantaged schools are likely to be better resourced than disadvantaged schools[1], as are general education schools compared to vocational schools. Figure 2.8 and Figure 2.9 show that these trends are also true in Western Balkan education systems; however, there are large differences at the system level. For example, principals of disadvantaged schools in Albania are much more likely to report shortages in material resources than principals who work in similar schools located in other Western Balkan economies. In terms of disparities across educational programmes, principals of vocational schools in Bosnia and Herzegovina are much more likely than vocational principals in other regional economies to report concerns about material resources.

Figure 2.8. Principals' perceptions of material resources in advantaged and disadvantaged schools

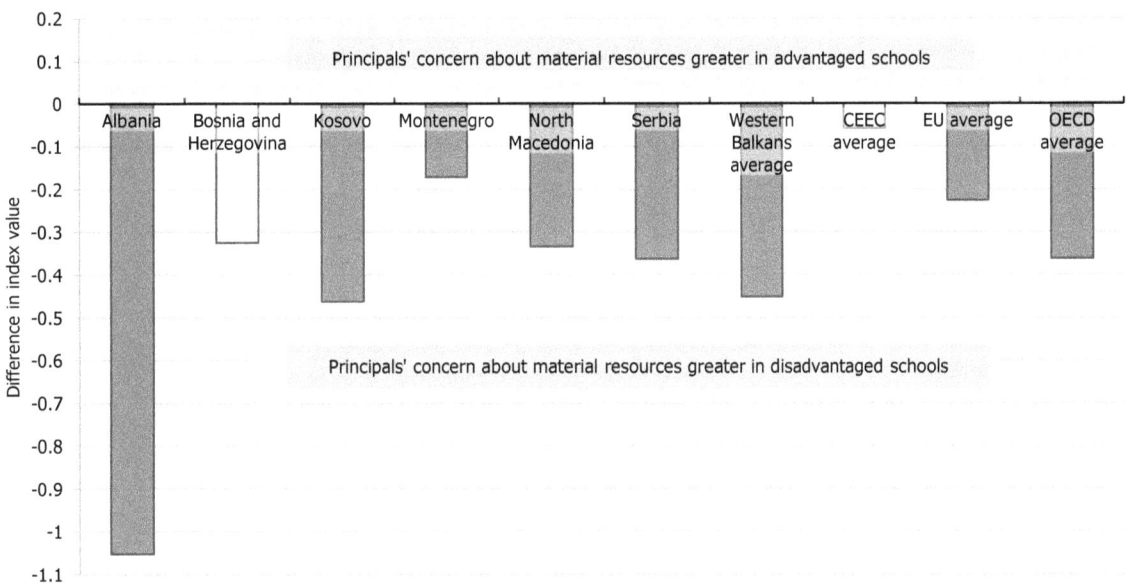

Note: Values that are statistically significant are shaded.
Answers to questions in Table 2.4 were used to create an index of concern about material resources. This index is calibrated such that the OECD average is zero, and a value of one represents one standard deviation away from the OECD average.
Source: OECD (2019[1]). PISA 2018 Database. https://www.oecd.org/pisa/data/2018database/ (accessed 17 November 2020).

StatLink https://doi.org/10.1787/888934199843

Figure 2.9. Principals' perceptions of material resources in general and vocational schools

Only principals from upper-secondary schools

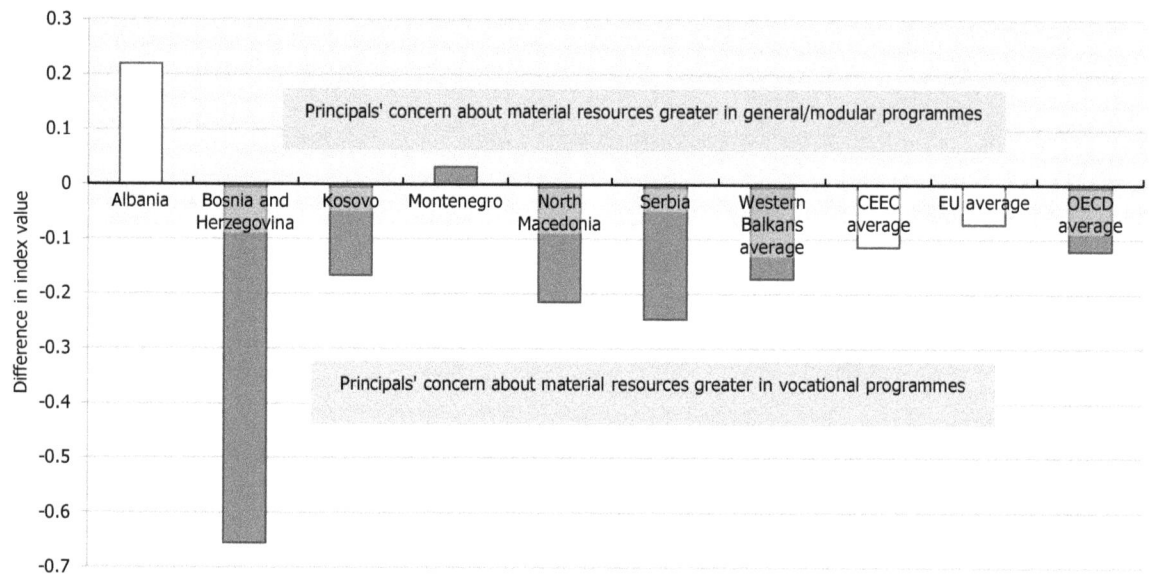

Note: Values that are statistically significant are shaded.
Answers to questions in Table 2.4 were used to create an index of concern about material resources. This index is calibrated such that the OECD average is zero, and a value of one represents one standard deviation away from the OECD average.
Source: OECD (2019[11]). PISA 2018 Database. https://www.oecd.org/pisa/data/2018database/ (accessed 17 November 2020).

StatLink https://doi.org/10.1787/888934199862

Similar to other types of material resources, technological infrastructure, and perceptions of its adequacy, is not allocated equitably across Western Balkan schools. The availability of technological infrastructure is crucial to modern education systems as it indicates the quality and relevance of educational provision in the digital age. Technology also enables distance learning when schools are not able to operate normally, such as recently during the school closures prompted by the COVID-19 pandemic.

As part of the PISA 2018 school questionnaire on educational materials, principals were asked a series of questions about their schools' technological infrastructure. Figure 2.10 and Table 2.5 show that schools in the region tend to have poorer technological infrastructure and, when these resources are available, they are often perceived as less sufficient. Figure 2.11 and Table 2.6 show that available technological resources are not distributed equitably. Advantaged schools tend to have more computers, a larger share of computers connected to the internet, and principals from advantaged schools are more likely to report having sufficient technological resources compared to principals from disadvantaged schools.

| 51

Figure 2.10. Technological infrastructure

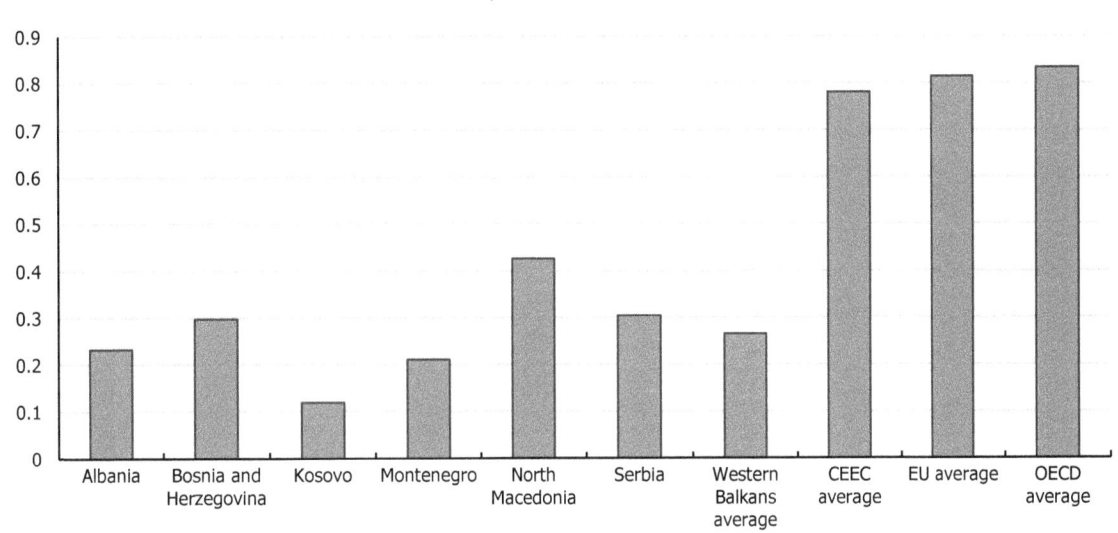

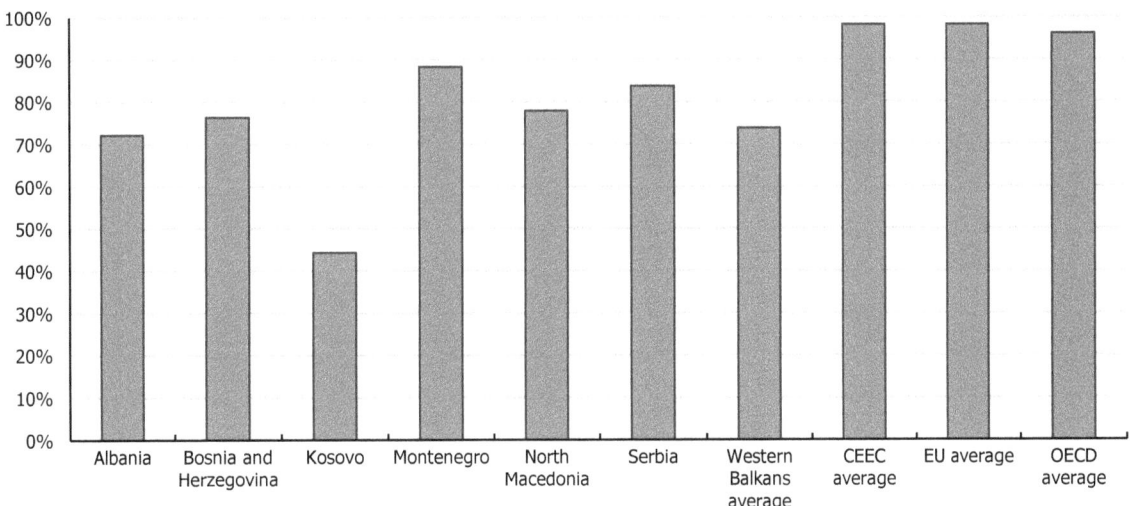

Source: OECD (2019[1]). PISA 2018 Database. https://www.oecd.org/pisa/data/2018database/ (accessed 17 November 2020).

StatLink https://doi.org/10.1787888934199881

EDUCATION IN THE WESTERN BALKANS © OECD 2020

Table 2.5. Principals' perceptions of technological infrastructure

Percentage of students in schools whose principal agreed or strongly agreed with the following statements:

	An effective online learning support platform is available	The number of digital devices for instruction is sufficient	The availability of adequate software is sufficient	Teachers have the necessary technical and pedagogical skills to integrate digital devices in instruction
Albania	32	38	47	89
Bosnia and Herzegovina	34	38	35	67
Kosovo	22	15	17	72
Montenegro	49	40	57	76
North Macedonia	24	38	44	79
Serbia	40	43	49	71
Western Balkans average	34	35	41	76
CEEC average	52	61	71	73
EU average	52	59	72	65
OECD average	54	59	71	65

Note: Darker tones indicate greater agreement.
- Less than 25
- 25 to 50
- 50 to 60
- 60 to 70
- Greater than 70

Source: OECD (2019[1]). PISA 2018 Database: https://www.oecd.org/pisa/data/2018database/ (accessed 17 November 2020).

StatLink https://doi.org/10.1787/888934199900

Figure 2.11. Technological infrastructure in advantaged and disadvantaged schools

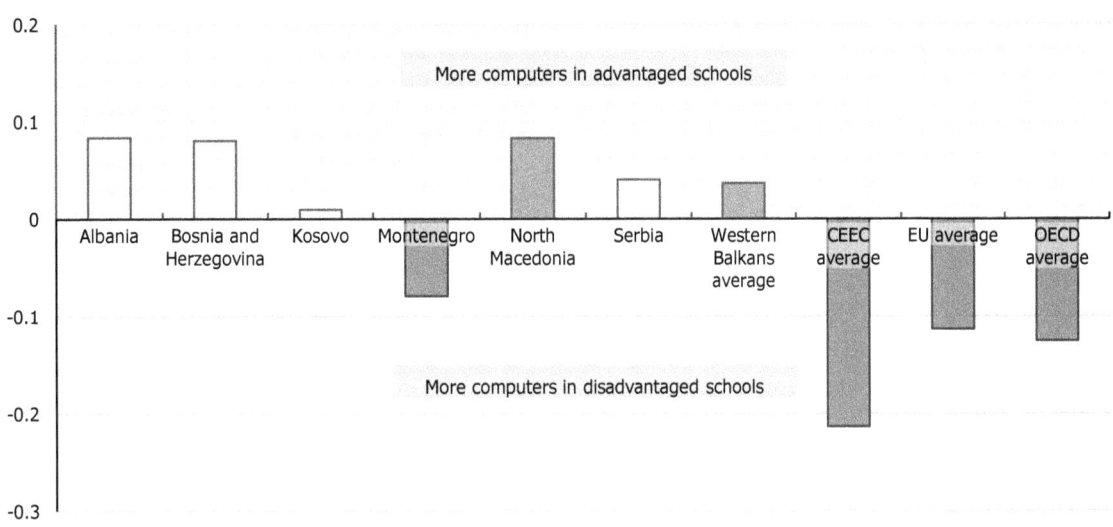

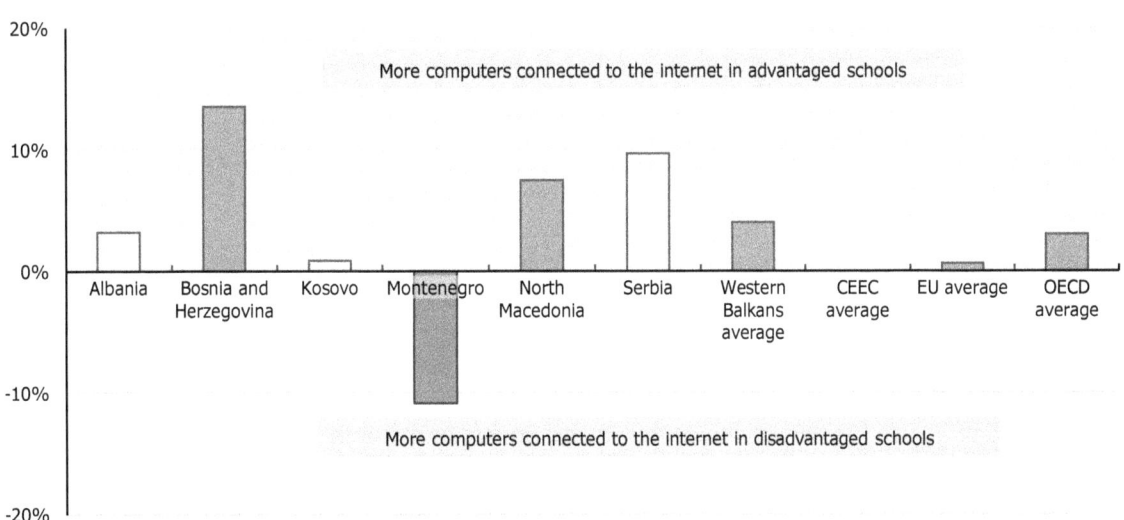

Note: Values that are statistically significant are shaded.
Source: OECD (2019[1]). PISA 2018 Database. https://www.oecd.org/pisa/data/2018database/ (accessed 17 November 2020).

StatLink https://doi.org/10.1787/888934199919

Table 2.6. Principals' perceptions of technological infrastructure in advantaged and disadvantaged schools

Difference in the percentage of students in schools (advantaged minus disadvantaged) whose principal agreed or strongly agreed with the following statements:

	An effective online learning support platform is available	The number of digital devices for instruction is sufficient	The availability of adequate software is sufficient	Teachers have the necessary technical and pedagogical skills to integrate digital devices in instruction
Albania	33	47	45	5
Bosnia and Herzegovina	19	10	10	-10
Kosovo	14	2	-12	11
Montenegro	-29	12	3	-9
North Macedonia	9	21	49	-22
Serbia	20	10	19	4
Western Balkans average	11	17	19	-3
CEEC average	0	1	3	1
EU average	8	5	9	6
OECD average	10	11	11	7

▓ Higher capacity in socio-economically advantaged schools
☐ Higher capacity in socio-economically disadvantaged schools

Source: OECD (2019[1]). PISA 2018 Database. https://www.oecd.org/pisa/data/2018database/ (accessed 17 November 2020).

StatLink ⟶ https://doi.org/10.1787/888934199938

Digital resource shortages, both real and perceived, are not necessarily related to student performance

Concerns about inadequate resourcing are typically connected with the belief that greater resourcing can produce stronger student outcomes. However, while schools and teachers undoubtedly need proper resources to educate students, simply providing resources is not enough to improve student learning. Those resources also need to be relevant to schools' needs and school staff need to have the capacity to use those resources. If these conditions are not met, then more resources will not necessarily lead to better outcomes and countries risk inefficiently investing limited educational funds.

According to data from PISA 2018, the relationship between more resourcing and better outcomes is not conclusive. This trend is true internationally and across Western Balkan economies. For instance, North Macedonia has the highest computer-to-student ratio in the region, likely owing to a recent initiative to provide one laptop per child (OECD, 2019[4]). However, there is no relationship in North Macedonia between the number of computers and student outcomes (Table 2.7). These findings further suggest that it is how resources are used, not just their availability, that helps determine whether they support student learning.

Table 2.7. School resources and reading performance

Association between reading performance and the following variables

	Shortage of material resources	Number of available computers per student for educational purposes	Percentage of computers connected to the Internet
Albania			
Bosnia and Herzegovina			
Kosovo			
Montenegro			
North Macedonia			
Serbia			
Western Balkans average			
CEEC average			
EU average			
OECD average			

	Percentage of students in schools whose principal agreed or strongly agreed that:			
	The number of digital devices for instruction is sufficient	The availability of adequate software is sufficient	Teachers have the necessary technical and pedagogical skills to integrate digital devices in instruction	An effective online learning support platform is available
Albania				
Bosnia and Herzegovina				
Kosovo				
Montenegro				
North Macedonia				
Serbia				
Western Balkans average				
CEEC average				
EU average				
OECD average				

Note: Results based on linear regression models, after accounting for the students' and schools' socio-economic status.
▪ Positive association
☐ Negative association
Source: OECD (2019[1]). PISA 2018 Database. https://www.oecd.org/pisa/data/2018database/ (accessed 17 November 2020).

StatLink https://doi.org/10.1787/888934199957

Policy implications

Adequate funding and re-distributive policies can enable more equitable allocations of educational resources

In order to direct resources to where they can make the greatest difference, many OECD and EU countries use a combination of allocation mechanisms that aim to address the needs of schools with the most marginalised population groups (e.g. students with disabilities and from disadvantaged backgrounds). These mechanisms typically take the form of additional funding provided to particular schools (e.g. by including weights based upon student characteristics in a funding formula) or through targeted programmes (e.g. grants), which are provided for specific purposes but are separate from main allocations

(OECD, 2017[11]). In the Western Balkans, some education systems have already started exploring similar approaches. Serbia, for example, has tried to develop a per-capita funding formula; however, implementation remains a challenge (Maghnouj, S., 2020[3]). Albania is providing grants to certain groups of students to cover costs of transportation to school and textbooks (UNICEF, 2017[12]). These types of re-distributive policies can help Western Balkan economies use their limited educational resources more equitably and efficiently.

Strengthening school evaluation can help identify and address the needs of individual schools

Ensuring effective resourcing requires first accurately identifying the strengths and weaknesses of schools. In this regard, school evaluation frameworks are crucial because they generate data about school needs that can help direct necessary resources and support. Similar to most OECD and EU countries, several Western Balkan economies have already developed school evaluation frameworks. Traditionally, these frameworks typically evaluated schools according to their compliance with rules and procedures but increasingly focus on how schools help students learn (OECD, 2013[5]). Serbia, for instance, has created a school evaluation framework with a set of school quality standards that emphasise teaching and learning practices and outcomes (Maghnouj, S., 2020[3]).

Successfully conducting school evaluations is difficult. An important aspect is whether the assessment of a school's needs is accurate and focuses on effective practice. Regional systems have adopted several strategies to improve their assessment of school needs. For example, Serbia introduced new school quality standards in 2012, which were further revised in 2018 following initial testing to focus more on effective practice. North Macedonia is overhauling its school evaluation framework so it focuses less on compliance, more on student learning, and strengthens the importance of self-evaluation so principals can exercise more instructional leadership (OECD, 2019[4]). Education systems can use this information to design more effective school improvement policies. In Serbia, school evaluation results have been used to facilitate peer-learning across high and low performing schools.

Building school leadership capacity can help schools use resources more effectively

Adequate resourcing will not necessarily produce the desired outcomes if school staff do not have the capacity to use those resources to help students learn. Central in this effort are school leaders, who are responsible for directing teaching and learning at their schools and overseeing how resources are used (Pont, Nusche and Moorman, 2008[13]). To ensure that principals are prepared to fulfil their important functions, many countries select principals based on their ability to help schools improve student learning, as opposed to their political affiliations or experience in other professions, and require that they undergo extensive training.

Most school principals in the Western Balkans were former teachers, which is positive because it ensures principals are familiar with the school environment. However, OECD-UNICEF policy reviews have found that school principals in the region tend to view their role as administrative rather than as instructional leaders responsible for planning and driving school improvement. Moreover, the profession is often characterised by political interference in hiring processes and limited training opportunities. These factors contribute to creating cadres of school leaders that are not always well equipped to improve teaching and learning at their schools.

Several Western Balkan economies have started addressing these issues by making principal appointments more transparent and offering more substantial and relevant preparation for principals. For example, in 2017 Albania established a School of Directors as a centre for educational leadership (Maghnouj, S., 2020[2]); and in North Macedonia, prospective principals must pass a certification and licensing examination that assesses computer skills, theoretical knowledge and includes a presentation of a seminar paper (OECD, 2019[4]). These initiatives offer promising examples for how other systems in the region can strengthen the instructional and managerial capacity needed for school leaders to manage schools and use resources effectively and efficiently.

School networks

Many OECD and European school systems are experiencing significant demographic shifts, which, along with other social and economic changes, is altering the landscape of school networks[2]. Specifically, birth rates are declining and rural communities are shrinking while urban populations grow. Western Balkan economies are grappling with similar challenges. Birth rates have declined since 2000, especially in Kosovo and Albania. There has also been extensive migration outflows and internal mobility from rural to more urban areas as families and individuals search for better work and educational opportunities (Table 2.8). These factors create challenges for regional development and the provision of public services, especially in the education sector. In particular, the overall number of students is decreasing in rural schools, creating unsustainable excess capacity, while schools located in cities are becoming overcrowded and struggling to accommodate increased demand (OECD, 2018[14]; Maghnouj, S., 2020[2]; Maghnouj, S., 2020[3]; OECD, 2019[4]).

Demographic pressures are even more consequential in Western Balkan education systems because several economies in the region already have extended networks of small schools catering to students with different linguistic backgrounds (see Chapter 1). Governance arrangements in some parts of the region also lead to significant issues in terms of the jurisdiction, responsibility and co-ordination of education policy. These circumstances can make it difficult for education authorities in the Western Balkans to provide high quality and equitable teaching and learning opportunities across territorial spaces and linguistic groups.

Table 2.8. Changes in demographic indicators from 2000 to 2018

Value in 2018 minus value in 2000

	Birth rate (per 1,000 people)	Urban population as a percentage of total population
Albania	-4.6	18.6
Bosnia and Herzegovina	-2.9	5.9
Kosovo	-6.8	Data not available
Montenegro	-2.0	8.3
North Macedonia	-2.2	-0.6
Serbia	-0.6	3.3
EU average	-1.0	3.7
OECD average	-2.3	4.9

Source: World Bank (2020[15]). Fertility rate, total (births per woman). https://data.worldbank.org/indicator/SP.DYN.TFRT.IN (accessed 17 November 2020).

Data from PISA

School sizes vary widely both across and within Western Balkan education systems

Overall, data from PISA reveal that 15 year-old students in the Western Balkans attend schools that are similar in size to schools internationally. However, large deviations are observed at the system level (Figure 2.12). Albania and Bosnia and Herzegovina, for example, have especially large numbers of very small schools. The smallest 10% of upper-secondary schools in Bosnia and Herzegovina have fewer than

84 students, much lower than the smallest upper-secondary schools across the OECD, which have fewer than 339 students. On the other hand, the largest 10% of upper-secondary schools in Kosovo have over 1 750 students, substantially larger than the largest schools across EU countries (1281). Nevertheless, the smallest 10% of schools in Kosovo are similar in size to the smallest schools in the EU, suggesting that Kosovo has a very wide range of school sizes.

The disparity in school size implies diverse challenges for school networks. Small schools are often under resourced and less cost effective, but may stay open in order to provide access to compulsory education for students living in remote areas or, in some cases, to ensure that different linguistic have access to instruction in their mother tongues. On the other hand, while larger urban schools can benefit from economies of scale, staff in these schools may have less time to dedicate to each student and schools in these contexts often serve students from heterogeneous backgrounds, presenting challenges for individualised instruction and classroom management.

Figure 2.12. School size across the Western Balkans

Only students in upper-secondary school

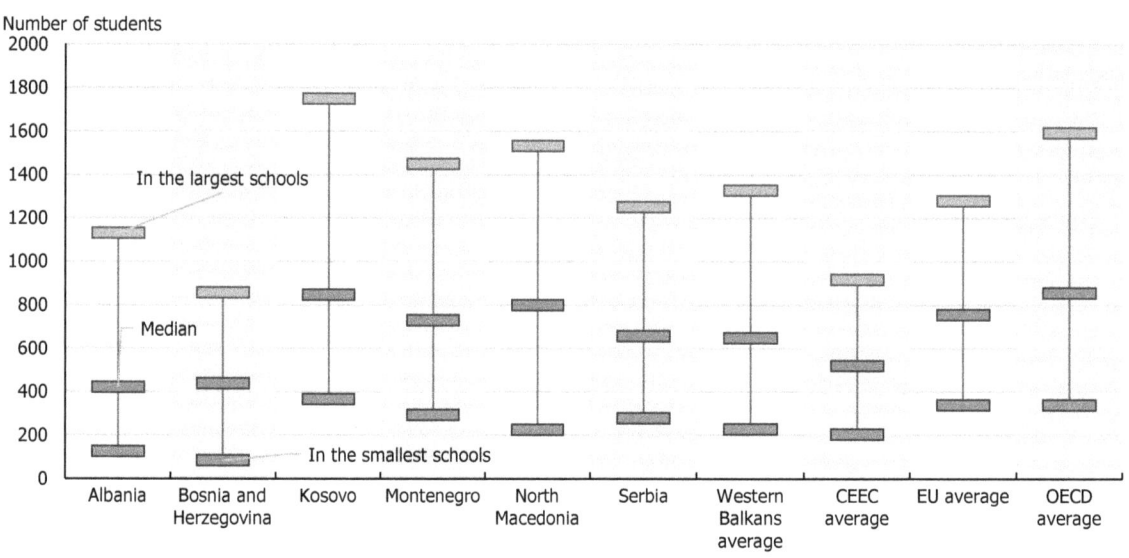

Note: Largest and smallest schools are defined as the top and bottom 10% of schools in terms of student enrolment.
Schools are weighted by the number of 15-year-old students enrolled.
Source: OECD (2019[1]). PISA 2018 Database. https://www.oecd.org/pisa/data/2018database/ (accessed 17 November 2020).

StatLink https://doi.org/10.1787/888934199976

Low student-teacher ratios affect school network efficiency

Partly owing to the large number of small schools, data from PISA reveals that student-teacher ratios in the Western Balkans have a much wider range than international averages. The difference between schools with the highest 10% and lowest 10% of student-teacher ratios in the Western Balkans is 12 students, compared with roughly eight students across EU countries. There are also notable variations within individual economies. Schools with the lowest 10% of student-teacher ratios in Bosnia and Herzegovina have fewer than three students per teacher, while the lowest 10% of schools in North Macedonia have fewer than five students per teacher. Both figures are substantially lower than the lowest 10% of OECD schools, which have fewer than nine students per teacher. When considering non-teaching staff, some of these schools in Bosnia and Herzegovina and North Macedonia could actually have more staff than students.

Data from PISA, however, suggest that neither smaller school sizes nor lower student-teacher ratios are related to improvements in learning outcomes. In fact, they are sometimes associated with lower student outcomes, which is likely related to the fact that small schools are more likely to be located in more rural areas, which tend to be poorer and face other disadvantages (Figure 2.13). Considering the high fixed costs of teacher salaries and the inconclusive evidence about staff size and student performance, maintaining large numbers of teachers in shrinking schools represents a major concern in the region. This situation is especially problematic given that Western Balkan education systems already face low levels of overall funding.

Figure 2.13. Student-teacher ratios

Only students in upper-secondary school

Note: Schools with the highest and lowest ratios are defined as the top and bottom 10% of schools in terms of student-teacher ratios. Schools are weighted by the number of 15-year-old students enrolled.
Source: OECD (2019[1]). PISA 2018 Database. https://www.oecd.org/pisa/data/2018database/ (accessed 17 November 2020).

StatLink https://doi.org/10.1787/888934199995

Table 2.9. Relationship between school network characteristics and student performance in reading

After accounting for student socio-economic status

	Smaller school size	Smaller student-teacher ratio
Albania		
Bosnia and Herzegovina		
Kosovo		
Montenegro		
North Macedonia		
Serbia		

Note: Results based on linear regression models, after accounting for the students' and schools' socio-economic status.
☐ Negative relationship
☐ No relationship
Source: OECD (2019[1]). PISA 2018 Database. https://www.oecd.org/pisa/data/2018database/ (accessed 17 November 2020).

StatLink https://doi.org/10.1787/888934200014

Policy implications

Rationalising school networks and classrooms can improve the efficiency and effectiveness of educational provision

A critical consideration for education authorities in the Western Balkans is how to provide quality teaching and learning opportunities across geographic areas and sub-sectors (e.g. schools that instruct in different languages) of the system. There are several ways to enhance the efficiency of school networks and a common approach used by several OECD and EU economies is consolidation. This method involves closing some schools and transferring their students to another site, which can increase school size but make education provision more efficient and effective (OECD, 2018[14]). Since some Western Balkan education systems allocate funding based on structural inputs (e.g. the number of classes within a school), there are limited financial incentives for schools to consolidate, as schools with larger classes would not necessarily receive additional funding. Devising school funding formulas based upon student enrolment, and in consideration of different student needs, which is occurring in Serbia and Albania, can help encourage consolidation where it is possible. Also helpful is demonstrating to parents and communities the benefits for students in accessing larger, better resourced schools.

In some rural communities and ethnic communities consolidation will be difficult to implement because students would then live too far away from a suitable school. In these and other situations, Western Balkan education systems have devised different means to increase the cost effectiveness of school systems. For example, Serbia and Albania operate satellite schools, whereby a central school runs a cluster of other schools to pool administrative and staff costs (Maghnouj, S., 2020[2]; Maghnouj, S., 2020[3]). In Bosnia and Herzegovina - which has some of the smallest schools in the region – some education authorities make use of multi-grade schooling. This practice involves students from different grade levels sharing the same classroom and teacher at the same time, which eliminates the need to have two teachers teaching very small classes. While similar practices can be found in other developing education systems and even OECD and EU countries, the effects of such approaches are highly dependent on the preparation and support teachers receive when working in these challenging circumstances (OECD, 2018[14]).

In the case of larger schools located in urban areas with high population density, schools sometimes operate in double or even triple shifts to accommodate a greater number of students. Kosovo and North Macedonia, which have some of the largest schools in the region, make use of multi-shift schedules. While this approach allows for highly efficient use of school facilities, it is important to consider the effects multi-shift schooling can have on the quality and time of instruction, as it could lead to more stressful learning environments, shorter break periods and increases in out-of-school class work (OECD, 2018[14]).

References

International Monetary Fund (2017), *Montenegro: Selected Issues*, https://www.imf.org/~/media/Files/Publications/CR/2017/cr17277.ashx. [9]

Kosovo Ministry of Education, S. (2016), *Kosovo Education Strategic Plan 2017-2021*, http://www.kryeministri-ks.net/repository/docs/KOSOVO_EDUCATION_STRATEGIC_PLAN.pdf (accessed on 20 March 2020). [8]

Maghnouj, S., E. (2020), *OECD Reviews of Evaluation and Assessment in Education: Albania*, OECD Publishing, Paris, https://doi.org/10.1787/d267dc93-en (accessed on 2 June 2020). [2]

Maghnouj, S., E. (2020), *OECD Reviews of Evaluation and Assessment in Education: Serbia*, OECD Publishing, Paris, https://doi.org/10.1787/225350d9-en. [3]

OECD (2019), *OECD Reviews of Evaluation and Assessment in Education: North Macedonia*, OECD Publishing, Paris, https://doi.org/10.1787/079fe34c-en. [4]

OECD (2019), *PISA 2018 Database*, https://www.oecd.org/pisa/data/2018database/ (accessed on 17 November 2020). [1]

OECD (2018), *Responsive School Systems: Connecting Facilities, Sectors and Programmes for Student Success*, OECD Reviews of School Resources, OECD Publishing, Paris, https://dx.doi.org/10.1787/9789264306707-en. [14]

OECD (2017), *The Funding of School Education: Connecting Resources and Learning*, OECD Reviews of School Resources, OECD Publishing, Paris, https://dx.doi.org/10.1787/9789264276147-en. [11]

OECD (2013), *Synergies for Better Learning*, OECD, http://dx.doi.org/10.1787/9789264190658-en. [5]

OECD (2010), *Learning for Jobs*, OECD Publishing, https://doi.org/10.1787/20777736. [6]

Pont, B., D. Nusche and H. Moorman (2008), *Improving School Leadership - Volume 1: Policy and Practice,*, OECD Publishing, Paris, https://www.oecd.org/education/school/improvingschoolleadership-volume1policyandpracticevolume2casestudiesonsystemleadership.htm (accessed on 20 January 2020). [13]

UNESCO-UIS (n.d.), *Government expenditure on education as a percentage of GDP*, 2018, http://data.uis.unesco.org/# (accessed on 20 March 2020). [10]

UNICEF (2017), *Albania: The cost of under-investment in education and ways to reduce it*, https://www.unicef.org/albania/media/451/file/The%20Cost%20of%20Underinvestment%20in%20Education%20and%20ways%20to%20reduce%20it.pdf (accessed on 8 September 2020). [12]

World Bank (2020), *Fertility rate, total (births per woman)*, https://data.worldbank.org/indicator/SP.DYN.TFRT.IN (accessed on 17 November 2020). [15]

World Bank (2019), *Republic of North Macedonia Public Finance Review: Sowing the Seeds of a Sustainable Future*, http://documents1.worldbank.org/curated/en/159301557513724528/pdf/North-Macedonia-Public-Finance-Review-Sowing-the-Seeds-of-a-Sustainable-Future.pdf (accessed on 9 September 2020). [7]

Notes

[1] A socio-economically disadvantaged (advantaged) school is a school in the bottom (top) quarter of the index of ESCS in the relevant country/economy.

[2] School networks refer to the location, size and offer of educational facilities in an education system.

3 Assuring high quality teaching

Introduction

Research has repeatedly suggested that, in terms of educational inputs, the quality of teaching is one of the most important factors in improving student outcomes (Hanushek, 2011[1]; Hattie, 2009[2]; Rivkin, Hanushek and Kain, 2005[3]). As a result, economies around the world, including those in the Western Balkans, have increasingly introduced policies that aim to improve the quality of teaching. Regional teaching reforms are wide reaching and varied, but broadly emphasise the need to use more modern teaching practices that have been shown to support learning for all students. To help achieve this goal, all economies in the region have created modern teacher standards that spell out expectations for teachers. These standards help inform initial teacher education, certification, appraisal and professional development by aligning institutions and practices around a new, shared vision of teaching.

This chapter uses PISA data to shed light on the types of practices that teachers in the Western Balkans commonly use to instruct students and to what extent they are consistent with system-wide expectations. It then examines how quality assurance mechanisms are functioning in the region and whether they might be reinforcing or complicating the implementation of the standards and desired teaching practices. By analysing these findings alongside insights from OECD-UNICEF policy reviews, this chapter also identifies policies that regional economies can consider to make teaching more effective.

Teaching practices

Teachers in the Western Balkans continue to rely heavily on traditional pedagogy, such as lecturing to students and encouraging them to memorise information set out in the curriculum. Research suggests that these practices, however, might not be as well-suited to developing some important competencies, such as those set out in recently introduced curricula in the region. In particular, international studies indicate that active, student-centred approaches might better help students develop so-called "21st century" competencies, such as creativity, critical thinking, collaborative problem solving and communication (Peterson et al., 2018[4]; Jacobs and Toh-Heng, 2013[5]). Moreover, traditional teaching practices can stand in the way of the personalised types of instruction that allow students to learn at their own pace and in different ways, which is especially important to make education inclusive regardless of factors such as gender and family background (OECD, 2012[6]). In response to these demands, many Western Balkan economies are taking steps to modernise teaching practices and adapt instruction to individual needs.

International experience shows that changing teachers' classroom practice can be very challenging. One reason education systems often struggle to implement modern practices is because providers of initial teacher education (ITE) might not equip teacher candidates to use new approaches. Many Western Balkan economies lack instruments, such as programme accreditation and robust certification requirements, which can help to align ITE with national teaching standards. Another reason is that more experienced teachers might be hesitant to adopt newer approaches or lack the support to do so. Many practising teachers were trained using very different pedagogical methods than what is expected of teachers today, and the former education culture of competition and selection of the communist period continues to influence teaching practices and beliefs. Evidence from PISA and OECD-UNICEF policy reviews indicate the extent of these challenges, as well as some of the ways in which they might be overcome.

Data from PISA

Pedagogical methods in the Western Balkans (as perceived by students) are still largely traditional and are associated with lower student performance

PISA 2018 can help illustrate the extent to which teachers in the Western Balkans are still using traditional pedagogical methods. The student background questionnaire of PISA 2018 asked several questions about instruction in reading classes, the responses of which comprised five indices about teacher practice (Table 3.1). All indices are calculated to have an average of zero and standard deviation of one across OECD countries. Positive values in the indices mean that students perceived their reading teachers to be more enthusiastic, provide greater support or use certain teaching practices more frequently than what was reported by the average student across OECD countries (OECD, 2019[7]). The adjusted results[1] for these indices are shown in Figure 3.1, which represents the extent to which each practice is more or less common relative to the others (and to the OECD average).

Table 3.1. Indices of teacher practice

Index name	Student prompt	Example questions
Teacher enthusiasm	Do you agree ("strongly agree", "agree", "disagree", "strongly disagree") with the following statements about the two language-of-instruction lessons you attended prior to sitting the PISA test?	It was clear to me that the teacher liked teaching us. The enthusiasm of the teacher inspired me.
Teacher support	How often ("never or hardly never", "some lessons", "most lessons", "every lesson") do the following happen in your language-of-instruction lessons?	The teacher shows an interest in every student's learning. The teacher gives extra help when students need it.
Teacher feedback		The teacher gives me feedback on my strengths in this subject. The teacher tells me in which areas I can improve.
Teacher-directed instruction		The teacher asks questions to check whether we have understood what was taught. The teacher tells us what we have to learn.
Adaptive instruction		The teacher adapts the lesson to [my] class's needs and knowledge. The teacher changes the structure of the lesson on a topic that most students find difficult to understand.

Source: OECD (2019[8]). PISA 2018 Database. https://www.oecd.org/pisa/data/2018database/ (accessed 17 November 2020).

Figure 3.1. Teacher practices

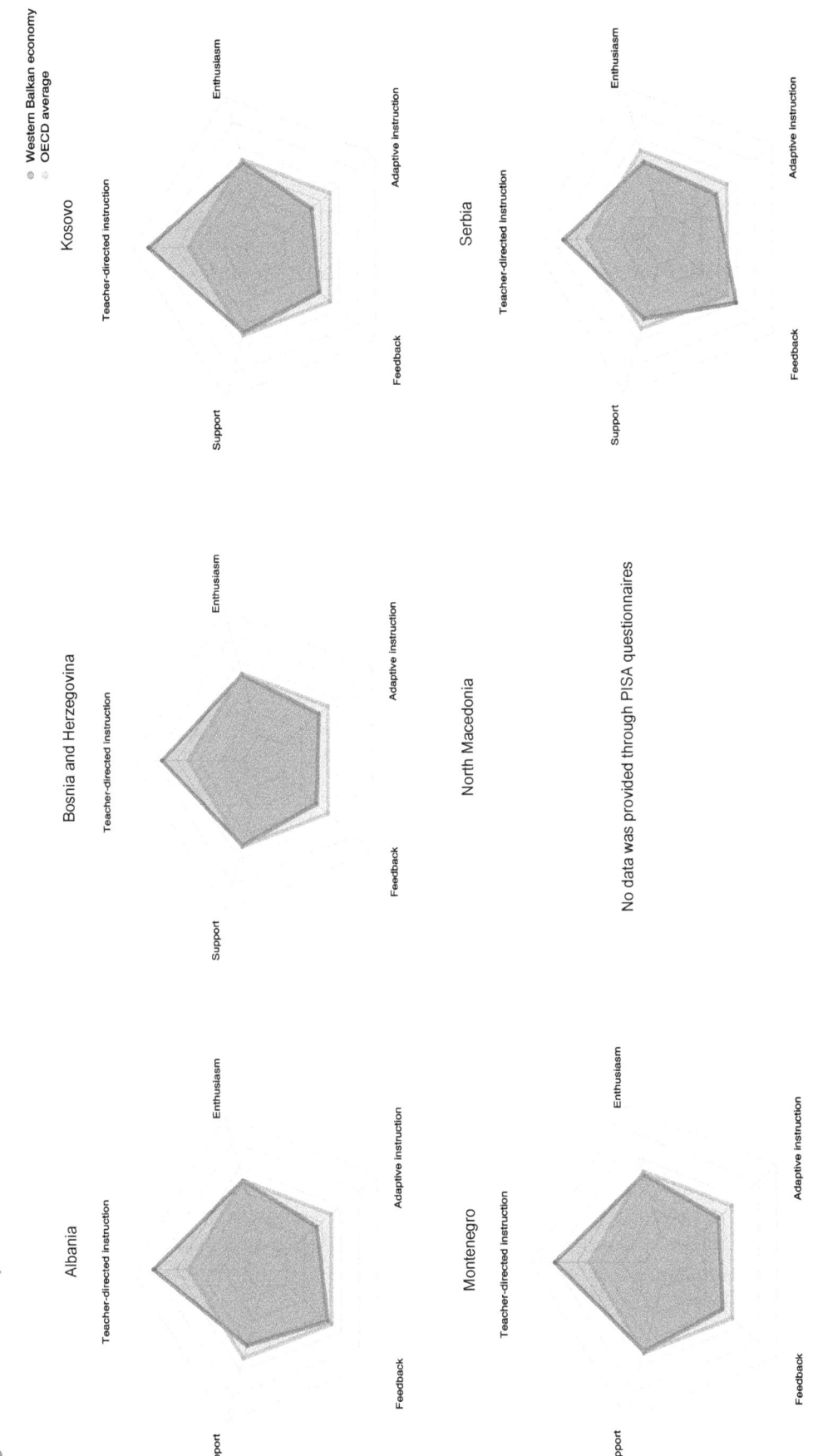

Source: OECD (2019[8]), PISA 2018 Database, https://www.oecd.org/pisa/data/2018database/ (accessed 17 November 2020).

Across all Western Balkan economies, data suggest that teachers are using less adaptive instruction and more teacher-directed instruction compared to OECD countries. This finding is important because students who reported a higher frequency of teacher-directed practices in language-of-instruction lessons tend to score lower in reading, even after accounting for gender and socio-economic status (Figure 3.2). In other words, teachers in the Western Balkans are less likely to use the practices that are more strongly associated with better student outcomes.

Figure 3.2. Teacher practices and reading performance

Change in reading performance associated with greater student reported exposure to:

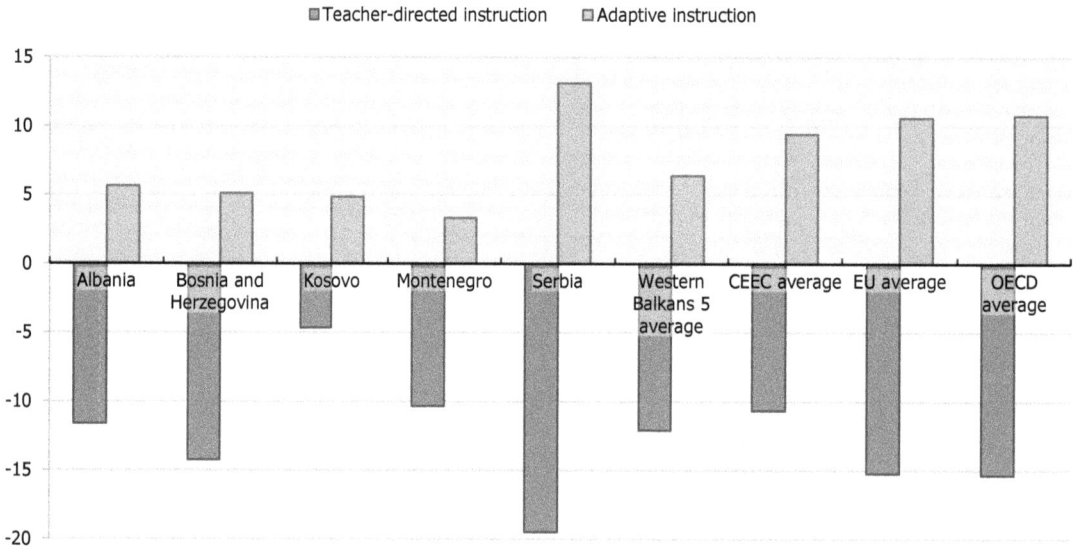

Note: Results based on linear regression analysis after accounting for gender and students' and schools' socio-economic status. All values are statistically significant.
Source: OECD (2019[8]). PISA 2018 Database. https://www.oecd.org/pisa/data/2018database/ (accessed 17 November 2020).

StatLink https://doi.org/10.1787/888934200033

Some teacher behaviours and practices may hinder student learning

Teachers not only have to be skilled in pedagogical methods, they also need to have the right outlook and mentality to work closely with students in potentially difficult environments. PISA 2018 asked school principals about the extent to which certain teacher behaviours and practices, such as teachers' resistance to change, unpreparedness, strictness and absenteeism, can create an unpleasant school climate and hinder student learning. Compared to international benchmarks, teachers in Western Balkan education systems consistently show higher rates of absenteeism and unpreparedness. In some systems, such as North Macedonia, principals also regard teachers as resistant to change (Figure 3.3). These findings raise important questions about why teachers might not be demonstrating professional behaviours, signalling the need to look more closely at teacher working conditions and pay and the adequacy of policies related to teacher accountability and ethical conduct.

Figure 3.3. Teacher behaviours and practices that may hinder student instruction

Percentage of students in schools whose principals reported that the following behaviours hinder student learning a lot

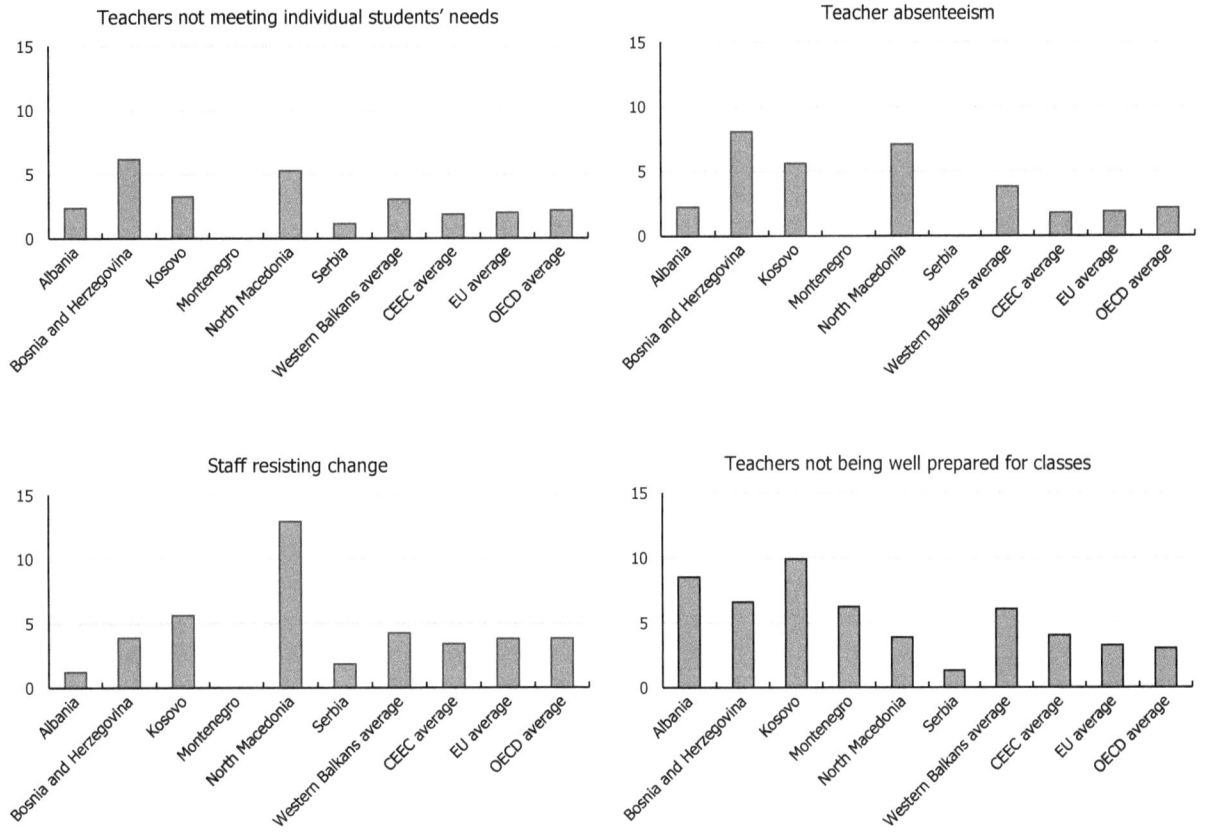

Source: OECD (2019[8]). PISA 2018 Database. https://www.oecd.org/pisa/data/2018database/ (accessed 17 November 2020).

StatLink https://doi.org/10.1787/888934200052

Policy implications

Teacher standards can help set out desired teaching practices

All Western Balkan education systems have created system-wide teacher standards to help guide the profession (Table 3.2). Most of these standards positively feature key pedagogical knowledge and skills and highlight important practices, such as individualised and adaptive instruction. However, findings from OECD-UNICEF policy reviews have revealed that there is often a lack of clarity about how teachers should demonstrate increased mastery of the standards over time. Moreover, there is rarely a clear relationship between the standards and career progression. For example, Serbia has a merit-based career structure for teachers but teacher standards are not used explicitly as a reference in promotion decisions, nor are higher levels of proficiency rewarded with higher pay (Maghnouj et al., 2020[9]). This disconnect limits teachers' incentive to continuously develop their practice. Providing more detail about core teaching competencies, setting out a road map for how they can be developed, and linking greater mastery with progress along the teacher career path (reflected in both differentiated roles and remuneration) will be important if teacher standards in the Western Balkans are to be used effectively as a lever for reform.

Table 3.2. Teacher standards in the Western Balkans

	Year when teacher standards were introduced
Albania	2013, revised in 2016
Bosnia and Herzegovina	2016-17 (inconsistently implemented)
Kosovo	2004, revised in 2017
Montenegro	2016
North Macedonia	Developed in 2016, but not implemented
Serbia	2011

Sources: Rexhaj, Mula and Hima (2010[10]). Mapping policies and practices for the preparation of teachers for inclusive education in contexts of social and cultural diversity. https://www.etf.europa.eu/sites/default/files/m/C12578310056925BC125772E002C487E_NOTE85SBG9.pdf (accessed 8 September 2020).
European Commission/EACEA/Eurydice (2018[11]). Teaching Careers in Europe: Access, Progression and Support.
Montenegro Institute of Education (2017[12]). Competence standards for teachers and directors in educational institutions. http://www.zzs.gov.me/naslovna/168346/NACIONALNI-SAVJET-ZA-OBRAZOVANJE-USVOJIO-STANDARDE-KOMPETENCIJA-ZA-NASTAVNIKE-I-DIREKTORE-U-VASPITNO-OBRAZOVNIM-USTANOVAMA.html (accessed 8 September 2020).

Professional codes of conduct can complement teacher standards

To address behaviours that may hinder student learning, Western Balkan education systems can consider developing a code of professional conduct for teachers. Internationally, a growing number of education systems have developed a professional code for teachers, which accompany their teacher standards. For example, in Scotland (U.K.), the teacher code of conduct defines core principles and values for registered teachers and sets clear boundaries for professional behaviour (GTC Scotland, 2012[13]). Other education systems, including in Singapore, conduct interviews to assess teachers' motivation and temperament as part of the teacher certification process. These codes can help develop awareness among teachers about what the core values of the profession are and how they are expected to conduct themselves.

Establishing codes of conduct might be especially relevant in the Western Balkans because there are concerns about the integrity of processes around appointing and dismissing teachers. Relations with the teaching profession are also sometimes politicised, which can put teachers into uncomfortable partisan roles. A code of conduct might help protect teachers from having to assume such a position.

Consistent communication can help teachers feel more motivated to adopt reforms

Most countries in the Western Balkans have embarked on frequent, major changes to important components of their educational systems, in particular their curricula. Nevertheless, consistently changing the educational landscape can make teachers feel unsettled and reluctant to alter their practices according to the newest change. Explaining how new methods of teaching relate to the shift in focus in student learning from knowledge memorisation to higher order competencies, and also explaining why this matters for students and societies, can help encourage a change in teaching practices and attitudes. North Macedonia, which has seen regular changes to its curricula over the past five years and which has the highest regional rate of teacher resistance to change, used the launch of its OECD-UNICEF review to catalyse communications with educators and stakeholders. Other Western Balkan systems can consider similar actions to communicate the intent of reforms, encourage teachers to participate in policy development, and motivate teachers to align their behaviours around common goals.

Teacher certification and qualifications

There are several ways in which countries can help to make sure that teacher candidates have the competences needed to teach in the classroom. A common approach is to require that teachers hold a minimum educational qualification. While requiring teachers to have high levels of education does not necessarily imply higher quality teaching, most OECD and EU countries oblige teachers to have at least a bachelor's degree, though master's degrees are increasingly mandatory to teach certain subjects or grade levels. Other common approaches used to develop and validate the competences of new teachers include raising the quality of initial teacher education (ITE)[2] programmes, requiring ITE graduates to pass a certification examination and/or implementing compulsory probationary periods. Examples of these types of quality assurance mechanisms are present in the Western Balkans (Table 3.3). However, in many parts of the region, teacher certification and qualification requirements are not applied with sufficient rigour and consistency to improve teaching and learning outcomes.

Table 3.3. Requirements to become a fully certified teacher in the Western Balkans

In addition to completing ITE (for primary- and lower-secondary-level teachers without subject-level specialisations)

	Level of education	Passing a central examination after ITE	Completion of a probationary period	Passing a central examination after probation
Albania	Master		X	X
Bosnia and Herzegovina	Bachelor		X	
Kosovo	Bachelor		X	X
Montenegro	Bachelor		X	X
North Macedonia	Bachelor		X	X
Serbia	Master		X	X

Notes: Bosnia and Herzegovina's policies differ according to administrative authority. In all areas, teachers must pass an examination after probation, but the examinations are not centralised.
Albania has a one-year internship before a probation year. Candidates take two central examinations after their internship but before their probationary year.
Sources: European Commission/EACEA/Eurydice (2018[11]). Teaching Careers in Europe: Access, Progression and Support.
World Bank (2019[14]). Bosnia and Herzegovina: Review of efficiency services in pre-university education. http://documents1.worldbank.org/curated/en/719981571233699712/pdf/Bosnia-and-Herzegovina-Review-of-Efficiency-of-Services-in-Pre-University-Education-Phase-I-Stocktaking.pdf (accessed 8 September 2020).
Mehmeti, Rraci and Bajrami (2019[15]). Teacher professional development in Kosovo. https://www.keen-ks.net/site/assets/files/1467/zhvillimi_profesional_i_mesimdhenesve_ne_kosove_eng.pdf (accessed 8 September 2020).

Data from PISA

Teachers in the Western Balkans are less likely to be certified and hold a master's degree

To better understand the relationship between student performance and the certification and qualification of teachers, PISA 2018 asked school principals to report the number of teachers in their schools who are "fully certified by an appropriate authority", and the number of teachers who hold advanced qualifications[3]. The data show that, compared to teachers in OECD and EU countries, Western Balkan teachers are less likely to be certified and hold a master's degree (Figure 3.4). However, both indicators reveal significant variance among regional economies. In Bosnia and Herzegovina, almost 80% of teachers are reportedly certified, which is similar to the OECD average (82%) but much higher than Serbia's share (63%).

It is important to note that education systems define their own credentials for "full certification" in PISA, meaning that requirements can vary across systems. For instance, certification could signal that a teacher has received an ITE qualification, accumulated a minimum number of student-teaching hours, passed an exam, some combination of these criteria, or none of them.

Around the world, a growing number of countries have made holding a master's degree[4] a certification requirement (as only holding the degree is not sufficient to become certified), especially for upper-secondary teachers who are expected to have deeper content knowledge. This requirement is the case in Albania, where a master's degree is already needed to teach in many contexts and where 67% of teachers reportedly hold a master's degree (Figure 3.4). In comparison, on average 45% of teachers in the OECD hold a master's degree. However, overall in the region, PISA data reveal relatively low qualification levels, notably in Montenegro and Bosnia and Herzegovina, where less than 8% of teachers reportedly hold a master's degree.

Figure 3.4. Teacher qualifications

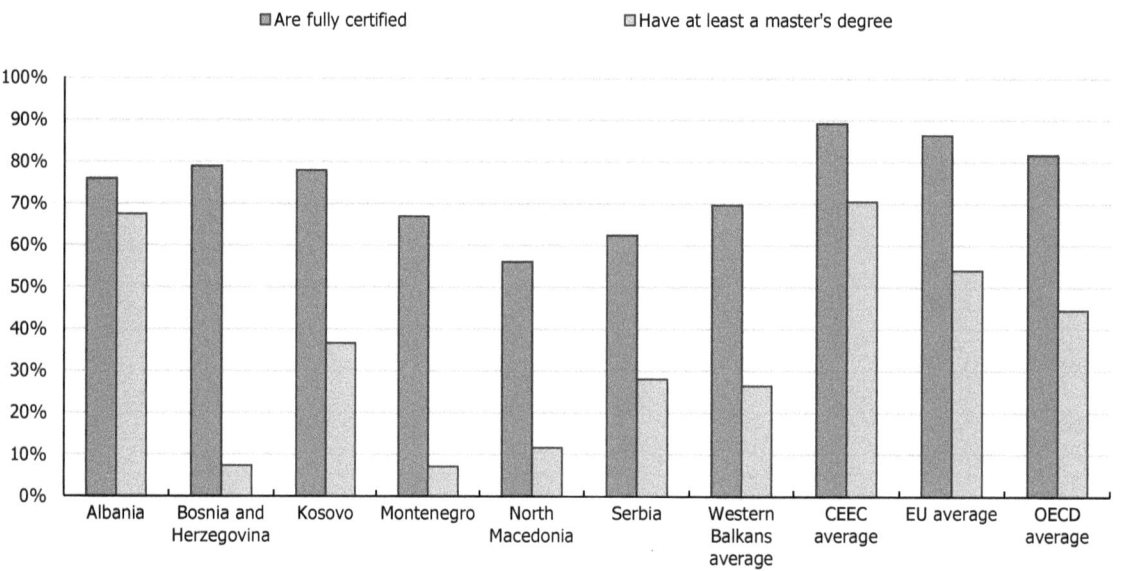

Note: Teacher certification in North Macedonia and Bosnia and Herzegovina is highly decentralised and in most cases consists of simply completing ITE. Given this context, it is possible that principals from these systems had difficulty interpreting whether their teachers were "fully certified" and thus North Macedonia's results should be interpreted with caution.
Source: OECD (2019[8]). PISA 2018 Database. https://www.oecd.org/pisa/data/2018database/ (accessed 17 November 2020).

StatLink https://doi.org/10.1787888934200071

Teachers with low educational qualifications could have implications for the effectiveness and professional status of the teaching workforce. However, what is more important than simply holding an educational qualification is the quality of the ITE programme that led to the qualification. Findings from OECD-UNICEF policy reviews reveal that many essential features of ITE programmes are not present in the Western Balkans. For example, while higher education accreditation processes exist in many parts of the region, ITE programmes usually do not undergo robust accreditation that is specific to teacher education and aligned with teacher standards (OECD, 2019[16]). Moreover, the length of the teaching practicum can vary within systems and there are few if any guidelines given to providers on how to design these programmes well (Maghnouj et al., 2020[9]). As a result, there is no way for educational authorities in the region to ensure effective quality control of the content and structure of ITE programmes.

There is no relationship between teacher qualifications and the use of modern practices or student outcomes in the Western Balkans

Implicit in policies about teacher qualifications is the belief that better qualified teachers help produce better student outcomes. Countries trust that quality assurance mechanisms, such as certification and educational requirements, reliably signal that a teacher is capable of helping students learn. Internationally, PISA data show that this signalling is generally accurate. Students from schools with greater shares of teachers who are certified and who have master's degrees tend to have higher performance, even after accounting for the students' and schools' socio-economic status. In the Western Balkans, however, the relationship is inconclusive or even negative (Figure 3.5). Furthermore, there is no relationship between teacher qualifications and the use of the modern teaching practices, even though such practices feature prominently in many regional teacher standards (Figure 3.6). These findings provide further evidence that certification and educational requirements in the Western Balkans are not sufficient and highlight the need for mechanisms that more accurately signal high quality teaching.

Figure 3.5. Teacher qualifications and student outcomes in reading

Change in reading performance for every 10% increase in the share of teachers who are:

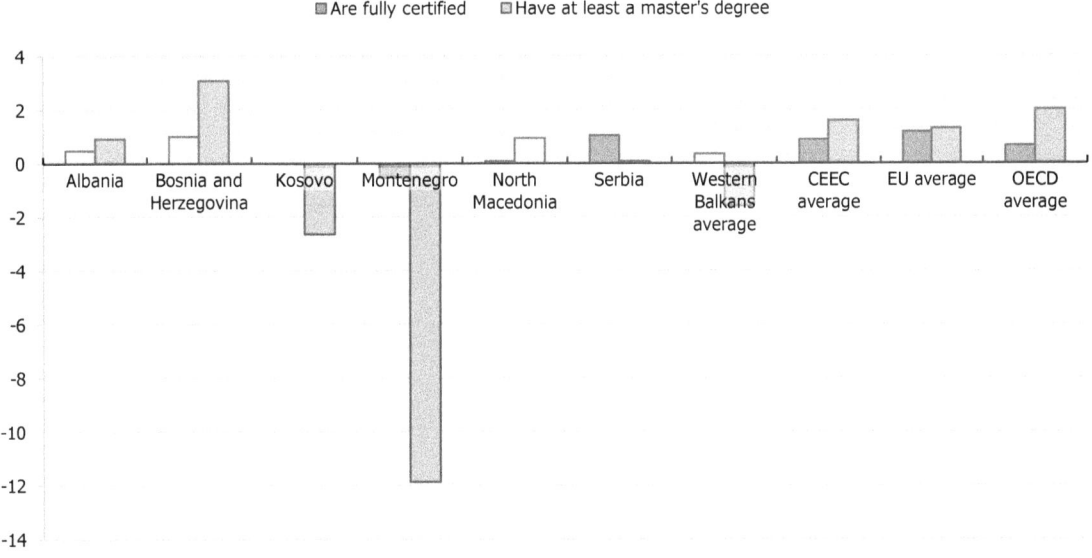

Note: Results based on linear regression analysis after accounting for students' and schools' socio-economic status.
Values that are statistically significant are shaded.
Source: OECD (2019[8]). PISA 2018 Database. https://www.oecd.org/pisa/data/2018database/ (accessed 17 November 2020).

StatLink https://doi.org/10.1787/888934200090

Figure 3.6. Teacher qualifications and teacher practices

Change in teacher practices for every 10% increase in the share of teachers who are:

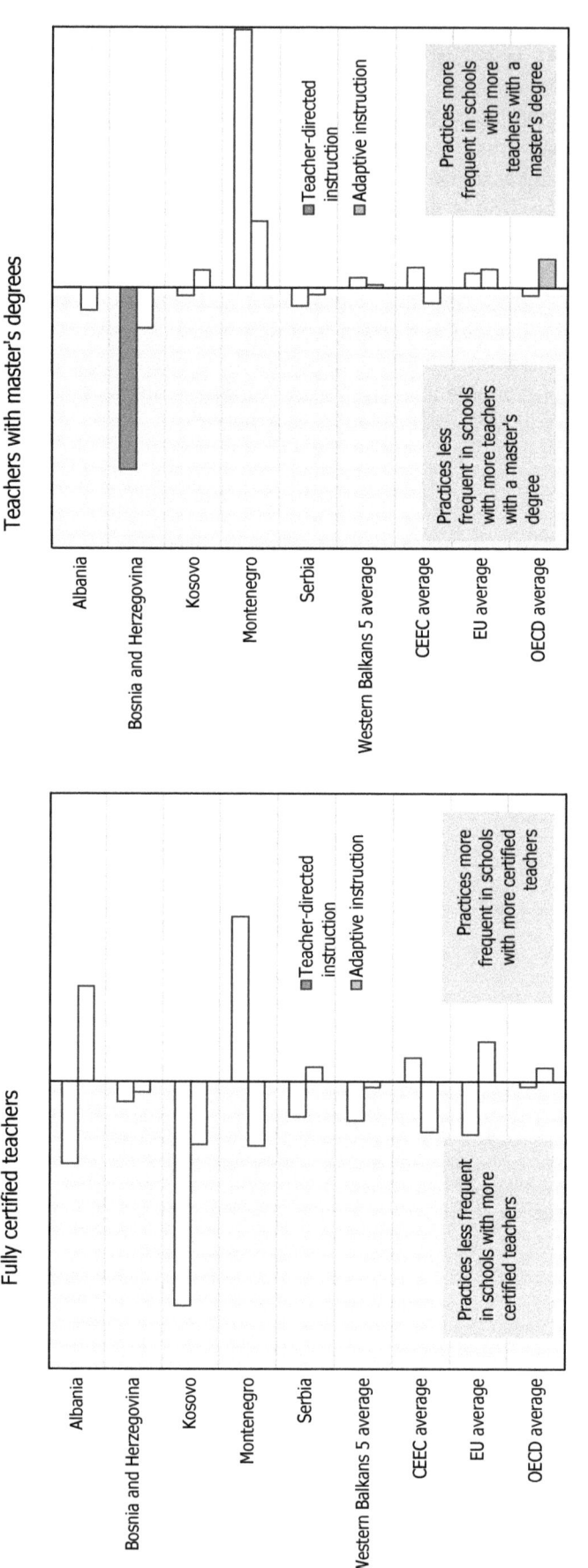

Policy implications

Raising the quality of initial teacher education programmes can help promote the use of modern instructional practices

Simply raising the minimum qualification needed to become a teacher is unlikely to improve teaching and learning outcomes in the Western Balkans if education systems do not simultaneously address the issues that are currently undermining the value and quality of ITE. Notably, all systems examined by OECD UNICEF policy reviews reveal that entry into regional ITE programmes is not selective, which is partly a reflection of the perceived status of the teaching profession in the region. This situation prevents authorities from ensuring that only candidates with strong academic skills and a clear motivation to teach are granted study places in ITE. Some economies in the region are already taking steps to strengthen ITE entry requirements, such as Albania, which has raised the prerequisite grade point average for entry into some ITE programmes (MoESY, 2018[17]). Another measure commonly used by OECD and EU countries to increase the calibre of ITE candidates involves conducting interviews to evaluate applicants' motivation and socio-emotional skills before granting them acceptance into ITE programmes.

Efforts to raise the bar for entry into ITE should be accompanied by measures to improve the quality of ITE programmes. However, findings from OECD-UNICEF policy reviews suggest that ITE programmes in the Western Balkans are often fragmented and vary in quality (OECD, 2019[16]; Maghnouj, 2020[18]). To address these issues, many OECD and EU countries have introduced specific guidelines and quality assurance mechanisms for ITE programmes. These measures typically set out mandatory accreditation criteria for ITE programmes that align with teacher standards (see above) and describe requirements related to the teaching practicum. Strong accreditation processes give ITE providers a common reference point around which to build their curricula and similar approaches could help Western Balkan systems raise the quality of ITE.

Rigorous certification processes can help signal high quality teaching

In addition to tightening regulations for ITE programmes, education systems can use certification to help improve the quality of ITE and ensure that all teacher candidates are ready to teach. An important feature of many certification processes, including those in the Western Balkans, is the use of examinations (Table 3.3). While examinations can influence the content of ITE programmes and help reinforce minimum standards for novice teachers, evidence from OECD-UNICEF policy reviews finds that certification examinations in the region tend to measure theoretical knowledge rather than practical pedagogy (Maghnouj, 2020[18]; Maghnouj et al., 2020[9]). As a result, certified teachers may enter the classroom with advanced understanding of an academic discipline, but unsure about how to impart that same understanding to their students.

To address some of the limitations of their certification examinations, all Western Balkan economies have introduced mandatory probation periods for new teachers. These periods are a positive feature of teacher certification in the region because they help verify some of the more practical aspects of teaching that cannot easily be measured by an examination. However, some of the elements that can support effective probation are missing, such as adequate time, support for beginner teacher mentorship, and clarity and rigour in the process for taking a final decision. Moreover, some systems in the Western Balkans administer certification examinations after the probationary period, rather than before teachers enter the classroom (Table 3.3). In a context where ITE quality assurance is weak, this measure can expose students to teachers who do not have a minimum level of competence. It can also focus the probation on passing an exam, rather than developing and demonstrating teaching abilities.

Teacher appraisal and professional development

Education systems need to ensure that teachers keep their skills up to date vis-à-vis system-wide goals. It is therefore crucial that teachers receive regular feedback about their practice and have access to meaningful and relevant professional development opportunities. Together, these efforts can help establish a coherent professional learning process that aligns with teacher standards and broader education goals. However, data from PISA and OECD-UNICEF policy reviews reveal that systems of teacher appraisal and professional development in the Western Balkans often struggle to encourage student-centred teaching practices. Without greater alignment of these policies, education systems in the region will likely have continued difficulty in improving teaching and learning.

Data from PISA

Teacher appraisal processes in the Western Balkans do not capture how well they help students learn

How teachers in the Western Balkans are evaluated might be hindering the adoption of more student centred teaching practices. Countries with well-balanced and formative teacher appraisal systems typically rely on a range of evidence[5] to make informed, qualitative judgements about how teachers support student learning. In the Western Balkans, however, education systems judge effectiveness according to the numbers of papers teachers present (as is the case in Albania), and the existence (but not quality) of teacher portfolios (as is the case in North Macedonia) (Maghnouj, 2020[18]; OECD, 2019[16]). These types of appraisal measures do not provide authentic and accurate indicators of teacher effectiveness because they measure a teacher's level of activity, but the completion of those activities does not necessarily indicate improved student learning.

An unusually common (when compared to international benchmarks) measure of teacher effectiveness in the region is student results in academic competitions (Olympiads) and summative tests (Figure 3.7). Compared to more authentic measures of teacher effectiveness, this metric is particularly problematic because it depends on students' background, their previous preparation and other circumstances that are beyond the teacher's control. Using student assessment results to judge teacher effectiveness can be especially unfair towards teachers who teach more disadvantaged students, and it could incentivise teachers to help high-achieving students excel rather than helping all students learn.

Figure 3.7. Using student assessment to appraise teachers

Percentage of students in schools whose principals report that student assessment results are used to appraise teachers

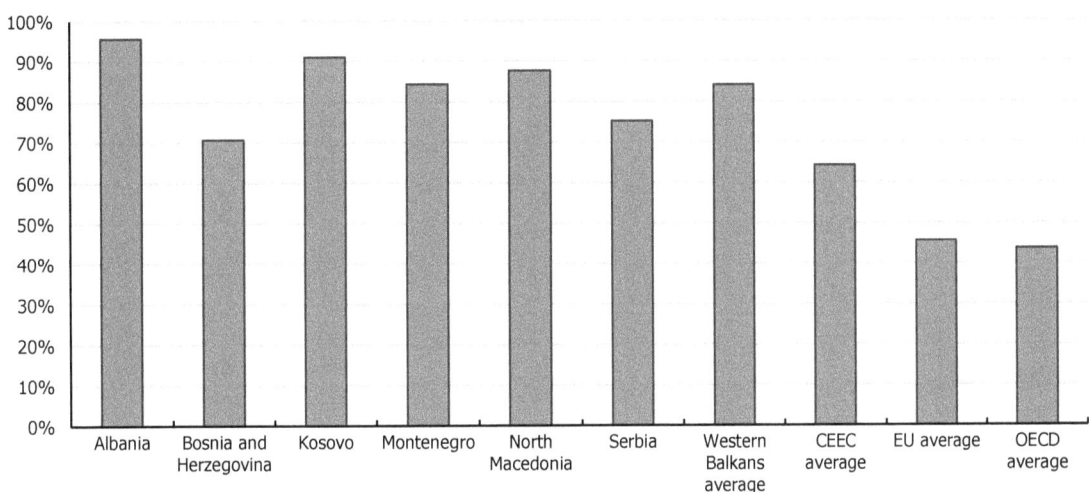

Source: OECD (2019[8]). PISA 2018 Database. https://www.oecd.org/pisa/data/2018database/ (accessed 17 November 2020).

StatLink https://doi.org/10.1787888934200128

Links between professional development and desired teaching practices are weak

Across the OECD, and especially in CEEC countries, data from PISA reveal a positive association between the amount of professional development teachers receive and how frequently they use adaptive instruction (Figure 3.8). However, these findings are less conclusive in the Western Balkans. While there is generally an association between more professional development and greater usage of adaptive instruction, the Western Balkans demonstrate greater variance both across and within systems, suggesting that the effectiveness of professional development may be inconsistent. These findings help explain why associations between professional development and adaptive instruction are not statistically significant. In some areas, teachers appear to be trained successfully in using adaptive instruction, while in others, often within the same economy, they are not.

Figure 3.8. Professional development and teacher practices

Change in teacher practices for every 10% increase in the share of teachers who participate in professional development

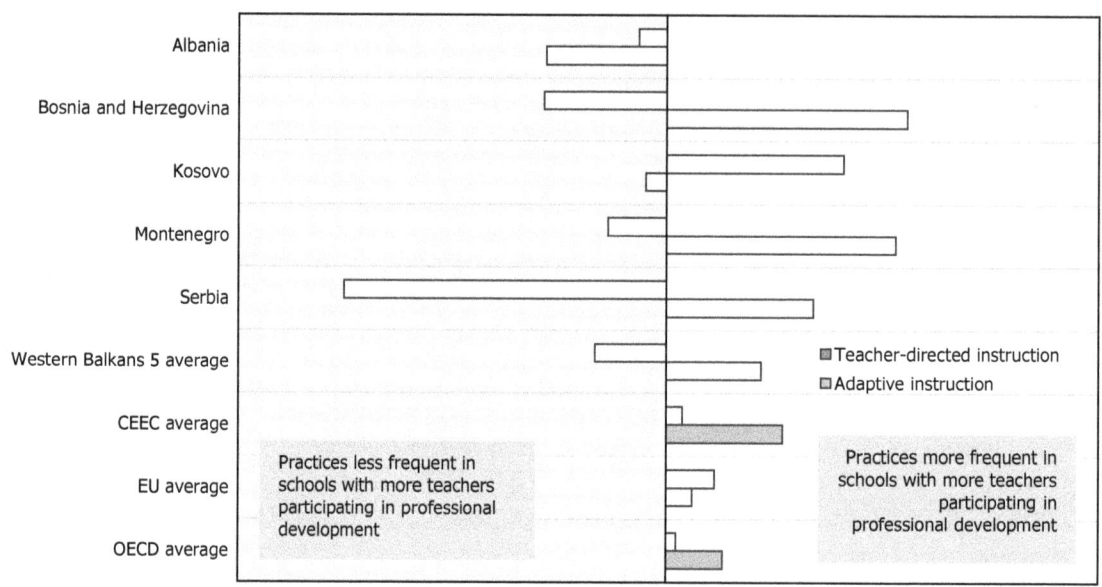

Note: Values that are statistically significant are shaded.
Source: OECD (2019[8]). PISA 2018 Database. https://www.oecd.org/pisa/data/2018database/ (accessed 17 November 2020).

StatLink https://doi.org/10.1787/888934200147

Findings from OECD-UNICEF policy reviews offer several possible explanations for these observed differences. Primarily, professional development in the region sometimes fails to address key gaps in teachers' knowledge and skills, such as understanding system-wide teacher standards and expected practices (OECD, 2019[16]; Maghnouj et al., 2020[9]). Some teachers might also have a hard time accessing professional development, either because they have little time to do so or because the relevant opportunities are not available to them (see following section). Finally, teacher appraisal in the region appears to further exacerbate these issues because current measures and evaluations of teacher effectiveness do not systematically inform teachers' professional development needs nor identify which teachers may need additional or specific training. As a result, teachers who may need support in using adaptive instruction might be trained in unrelated topics or not receive any training at all.

Teacher participation in professional development, and having the time to do so, varies across and within Western Balkan economies

An important question regarding professional development is to whom it is made available. Availability is particularly important for teachers who work in disadvantaged environments, as they might need more support to effectively teach their students. Results from PISA 2018 suggest that, on average, teachers in the Western Balkans participate in professional development, and are given opportunities to do so, at comparable rates to international benchmarks (Figure 3.9). Nevertheless, there is considerable variation across economies. In Albania, almost 70% of teachers participated in professional development in the three months leading up to PISA 2018, and over 80% have scheduled time to develop themselves, rates that are well above international benchmarks. In Kosovo, however, less than 20% of teachers recently participated in professional development, and in Bosnia and Herzegovina less than 30% of teachers have scheduled time to develop themselves, rates that are well below international benchmarks. These results suggest that, in many areas, much more can be done to ensure that teachers have time to develop themselves and have access to professional development opportunities.

Figure 3.9. Professional development

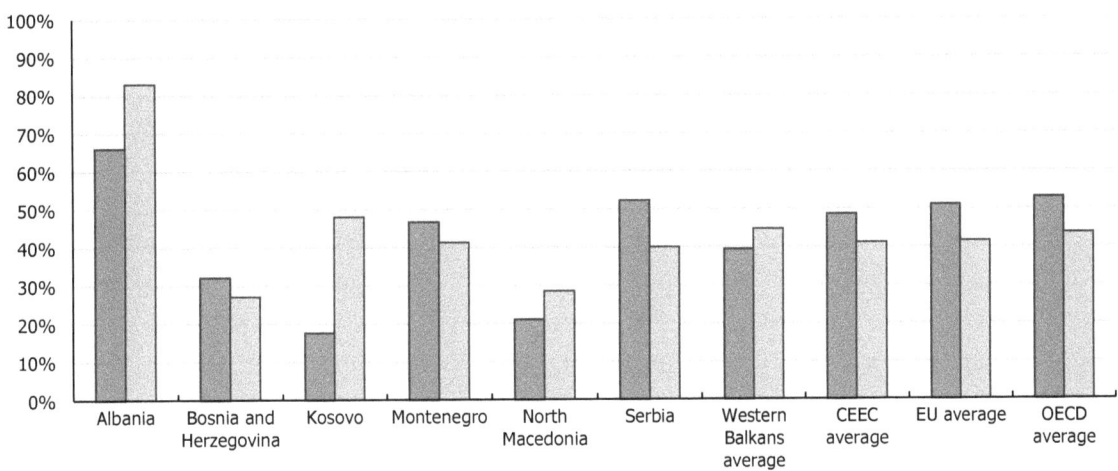

Source: OECD (2019[8]). PISA 2018 Database. https://www.oecd.org/pisa/data/2018database/ (accessed 17 November 2020).

StatLink https://doi.org/10.1787/888934200166

PISA data also show that there is significant variation within Western Balkan school systems in terms of teachers' access to professional development. Teachers who work in schools with more socio economically advantaged students are both more likely to participate in professional development and have more time to develop themselves than teachers in schools with more socio-economically disadvantaged students (Figure 3.10). In comparison, internationally, teachers in schools with more disadvantaged students are on average equally likely to participate in professional development and have time to do so. Across EU countries, teachers in schools with more disadvantaged students are actually more likely to participate in professional development.

In the Western Balkans context, teachers that instruct in different languages present a unique set of development challenges because they might need professional training in the different languages. PISA data show, in Bosnia and Herzegovina and in Montenegro, there are considerable differences in participation in professional development according to teachers' languages of instruction (Figure 3.11). These findings are worrying because they suggest that teachers who likely need more support are actually receiving less, which might exacerbate already concerning equity issues.

Figure 3.10. Professional development for teachers in schools with more advantaged and disadvantaged students

Difference between socio-economically advantaged and disadvantaged schools according to:

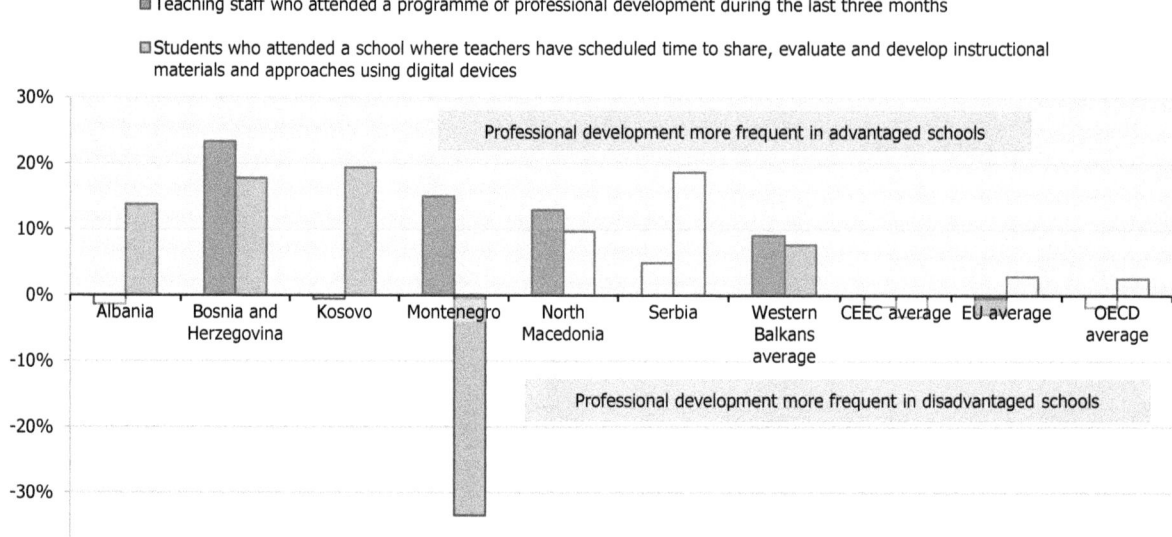

Note: Values that are statistically significant are shaded.
Source: OECD (2019[8]). PISA 2018 Database. https://www.oecd.org/pisa/data/2018database/ (accessed 17 November 2020).

StatLink https://doi.org/10.1787/888934200185

Figure 3.11. Teacher participation in professional development according to their languages of instruction

Teaching staff attended a programme of professional development during the last three months

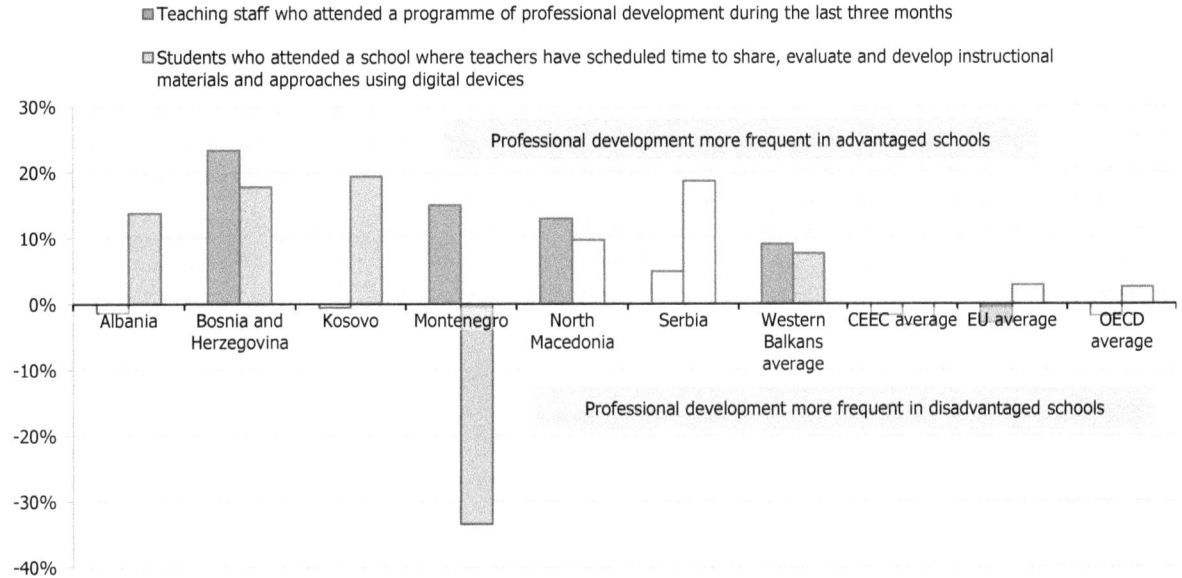

Note: Values represents shares from each linguistic group.
Source: OECD (2019[8]). PISA 2018 Database. https://www.oecd.org/pisa/data/2018database/ (accessed 17 November 2020).

StatLink https://doi.org/10.1787/888934200204

Holistic approaches to teacher appraisal can help promote desired teaching practices

Evidence from PISA and OECD-UNICEF policy reviews highlights the need to promote a more balanced approach to evaluating teacher quality in the Western Balkans. In particular, indicators and techniques used to measure teacher effectiveness need to go beyond student test scores and results in academic competitions. They should place greater emphasis on the quality of teachers' interactions with students and their ability to create an inclusive classroom environment where each student is encouraged to do his or her best. There are several policy options that Western Balkan systems can consider in order to promote more authentic measures of teacher quality.

First and foremost, the processes used to assess teachers and teaching practices – both by principals and external evaluation agencies – need to reinforce a more holistic approach. However, principals in the region typically lack central guidelines that help them evaluate teachers in ways that reflect teacher standards. In the absence of such guidance and support, principals may sometimes create their own appraisal criteria or fall back on familiar techniques (i.e. using student test scores). This situation risks that teachers' strengths and weaknesses are not correctly identified, which could lead to a misallocation of professional development resources and create equity issues with respect to where the best teachers can be found (Box 3.1). Developing central guidelines to help principals appraise teachers, which is underway in Albania, can help principals appraise teachers more authentically (Maghnouj, 2020[18]). Another way to improve the feedback teachers receive is to develop the instructional leadership skills of school principals. Albania's School of Directors, which was recently established as a structured programme for school principals, provides a promising example of this approach (MoESY, 2018[17]).

Education systems in the region also could align the rewards offered to schools and teachers with a more holistic understanding of teacher effectiveness. For example, current practices, such as giving bonuses to teachers and schools whose students perform well in Olympiads, do not promote more authentic measurement of quality teaching. Alternatively, regional education systems could require schools and teachers to demonstrate how they are helping struggling and disadvantaged students to succeed and bridging gaps in learning outcomes.

Box 3.1. Teaching practices in general education and vocational schools, and in advantaged and disadvantaged schools

Not being able to identify the best teachers can be problematic from the perspective of equity. Teaching in disadvantaged environments is challenging and, without suitable incentives, teachers might be hesitant to teach in schools with large shares of disadvantaged students. On the other hand, those same schools are where the very best teachers can contribute to student learning the most. Given these circumstances, it is vital that education systems be able to properly identify who the best teachers are so they can provide them with incentives to teach in difficult contexts.

In the Western Balkans, certification requirements, educational qualifications and teacher appraisal mechanisms are unable to reliably capture effective teaching practice. In the absence of this information, it is more difficult for education systems to ensure that all students have access to good teaching. PISA 2018 data show that the teachers who use adaptive instructional practices are distributed very inequitably throughout the region (Figure 3.12). In almost all economies, teachers who use more modern practices that are associated with higher outcomes are more likely to teach in general education programmes and advantaged schools, while teachers who use more traditional practices are more likely to teach in vocational programmes and disadvantaged schools. These findings are worrisome because they indicate that existing inequities are at real risk of being further exacerbated.

Figure 3.12. Teacher practices in general education and vocational schools

Only students in upper-secondary school

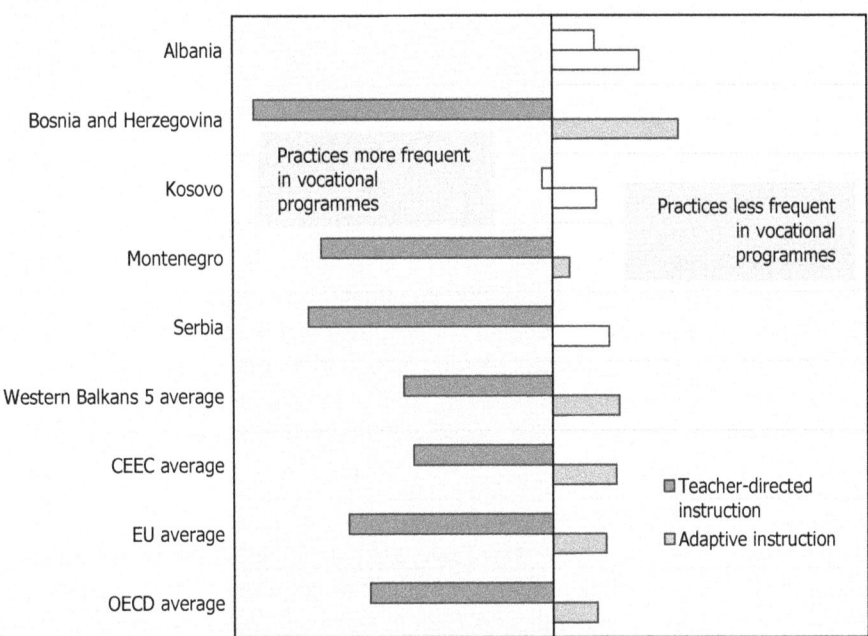

Note: Values that are statistically significant are shaded.
Source: OECD (2019[8]). PISA 2018 Database. https://www.oecd.org/pisa/data/2018database/ (accessed 17 November 2020).

StatLink https://doi.org/10.1787/888934200223

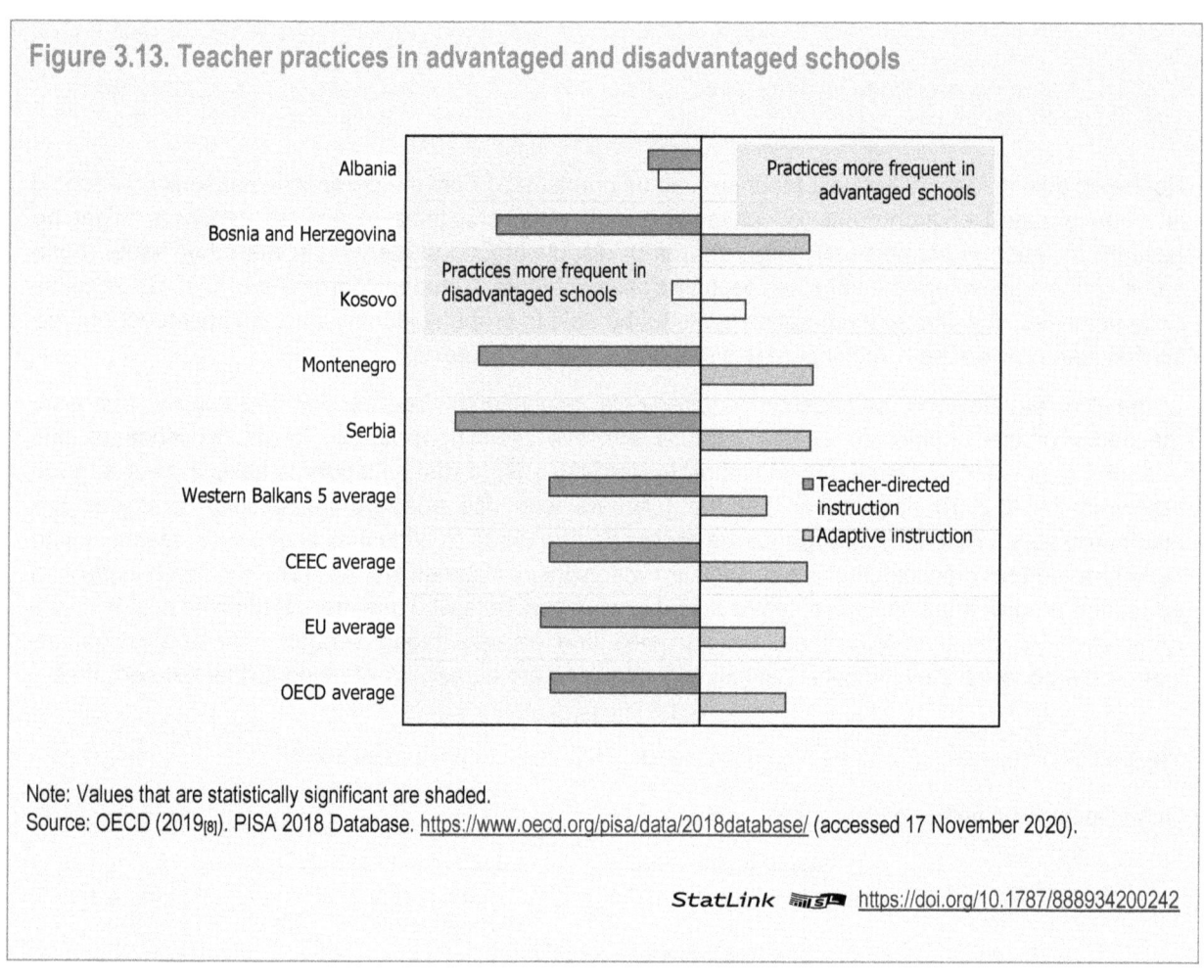

Figure 3.13. Teacher practices in advantaged and disadvantaged schools

Note: Values that are statistically significant are shaded.
Source: OECD (2019[8]). PISA 2018 Database. https://www.oecd.org/pisa/data/2018database/ (accessed 17 November 2020).

StatLink https://doi.org/10.1787/888934200242

Facilitating access to professional development opportunities can help teachers strengthen their practice, knowledge and skills

Findings from OECD-UNICEF policy reviews reveal that funding is one of the biggest barriers to the participation of Western Balkan teachers in professional development opportunities. While central and/or local governments usually provide some financial support, at least for priority training areas, these funds do not always cover the number of mandatory credit hours teachers must complete each year. Some teachers then have to cover the costs of formal training out-of-pocket, including transportation costs, which exacerbates inequity because teachers from more advantaged schools can more easily fund raise (Maghnouj, 2020[18]; Maghnouj et al., 2020[9]; OECD, 2019[16]).

In response to these challenges, some Western Balkan systems are introducing innovative methods for facilitating access to professional development for teachers. Serbia, for instance, is delivering professional development electronically, which makes it cheaper and more convenient for teachers to access training (Velickovic, 2020[19]). Albania has introduced professional learning networks, which provide teachers with training in national priority areas (though the use of a train-the-trainer method might be problematic given extant capacity concerns). North Macedonia requires schools to prepare four year professional development plans for teaching staff (OECD, 2019[16]) (Maghnouj, 2020[18]). While these approaches can help align school (and system) training goals, minimise expenditure and are considered effective ways to facilitate professional learning, resource-restrained Western Balkan systems should take care to avoid passing on full responsibility for professional development to schools.

Raising the quality and relevance of professional development opportunities can help increase teacher participation

Evidence from OECD-UNICEF policy reviews reveal that teachers who do participate in professional development do not necessarily demonstrate better practice. This finding suggests that in addition to facilitating access to professional development, education systems in the Western Balkans should take steps to make training offers more relevant and effective.

Western Balkan systems can consider several approaches to strengthening professional development. As mentioned, many Western Balkan economies require teachers to complete a set number of training credits each year. However, these requirements, when they are actually fulfilled, may lead to a box-ticking exercise whereby teachers participating for credit accumulation rather than for genuine learning and development opportunities. Basing career progression upon demonstrated evidence of helping students learn, instead of a raw count of completed activities, can help align professional development offerings with teacher interests and system-wide expectations.

Another method of assuring the quality of professional development opportunities is to establish accreditation procedures for providers. In North Macedonia, the government accredits training programmes through the Bureau for Development of Education. In Albania, the Quality Assurance Agency also accredits teacher training modules. These efforts can help teachers determine which programmes are considered to be high quality, which is even more important considering the resource limitations of the region.

References

European Commission/EACEA/Eurydice (2018), *Teaching Careers in Europe: Access, Progression and Support*, http://dx.doi.org/10.2797/708723. [11]

GTC Scotland (2012), *Code of Professionalism and Conduct*, The General Teaching Council for Scotland, Edinburgh, http://www.GTcS.orG.uk (accessed on 24 June 2020). [13]

Hanushek, E. (2011), "The economic value of higher teacher quality", *Economics of Education Review*, Vol. 30/3, pp. 466-479, http://dx.doi.org/10.1016/J.ECONEDUREV.2010.12.006. [1]

Hattie, J. (2009), *Visible learning : a synthesis of over 800 meta-analyses relating to achievement*, Routledge. [2]

Jacobs, G. and H. Toh-Heng (2013), "Small Steps Towards Student-Centred Learning", in *Proceedings of the International Conference on Managing the Asian Century*, Springer Singapore, http://dx.doi.org/10.1007/978-981-4560-61-0_7. [5]

Maghnouj, S. (2020), *OECD Reviews of Evaluation and Assessment in Education: Albania*, OECD Publishing, Paris, https://doi.org/10.1787/d267dc93-en (accessed on 2 June 2020). [18]

Maghnouj, S. et al. (2020), *OECD Reviews of Evaluation and Assessment in Education Serbia*, OECD Publishing, Paris, https://doi.org/10.1787/225350d9-en (accessed on 24 June 2020). [9]

Mehmeti, S., E. Rraci and K. Bajrami (2019), *Teacher professional development in Kosovo*, Kosovo Education and Employment Network, https://www.keen-ks.net/site/assets/files/1467/zhvillimi_profesional_i_mesimdhenesve_ne_kosove_eng.pdf (accessed on 8 September 2020). [15]

MoESY (2018), *Country Background Report: Albania*, Ministry of Education, Sports and Youth. [17]

Montenegro Institute of Education (2017), *Competence standards for teachers and directors in educational institutions*, http://www.zzs.gov.me/naslovna/168346/NACIONALNI-SAVJET-ZA-OBRAZOVANJE-USVOJIO-STANDARDE-KOMPETENCIJA-ZA-NASTAVNIKE-I-DIREKTORE-U-VASPITNO-OBRAZOVNIM-USTANOVAMA.html (accessed on 8 September 2020). [12]

OECD (2019), *OECD Reviews of Evaluation and Assessment in Education: North Macedonia*, OECD Publishing, Paris, https://doi.org/10.1787/079fe34c-en. [16]

OECD (2019), *PISA 2018 Database*, https://www.oecd.org/pisa/data/2018database/ (accessed on 17 November 2020). [8]

OECD (2019), *PISA 2018 Results (Volume III): What School Life Means for Students' Lives*, PISA, OECD Publishing, Paris, https://dx.doi.org/10.1787/acd78851-en. [7]

OECD (2013), *Synergies for Better Learning: An International Perspective on Evaluation and Assessment*, OECD Reviews of Evaluation and Assessment in Education, OECD Publishing, Paris, https://dx.doi.org/10.1787/9789264190658-en. [20]

OECD (2012), *Equity and Quality in Education: Supporting Disadvantaged Students and Schools*, OECD Publishing, Paris, https://dx.doi.org/10.1787/9789264130852-en. [6]

Peterson, A. et al. (2018), "Understanding innovative pedagogies: Key themes to analyse new approaches to teaching and learning", *OECD Education Working Papers*, No. 172, OECD Publishing, Paris, https://dx.doi.org/10.1787/9f843a6e-en. [4]

Rexhaj, X., M. Mula and A. Hima (2010), *Mapping policies and practices for the preparation of teachers for inclusive education in contexts of social and cultural diversity*, European Training Foundation, https://www.etf.europa.eu/sites/default/files/m/C12578310056925BC125772E002C487E_NOTE85SBG9.pdf (accessed on 8 September 2020). [10]

Rivkin, S., E. Hanushek and J. Kain (2005), "Teachers, Schools, and Academic Achievement", *Econometrica*, Vol. 73/2, pp. 417-458, http://dx.doi.org/10.1111/j.1468-0262.2005.00584.x. [3]

Velickovic, U. (2020), *Teacher training for using Microsoft Teams (Serbia)*, https://epale.ec.europa.eu/en/content/teacher-training-using-microsoft-teams-serbia (accessed on 8 September 2020). [19]

World Bank (2019), *Bosnia and Herzegovina: Review of efficiency services in pre-university education*, http://documents1.worldbank.org/curated/en/719981571233699712/pdf/Bosnia-and-Herzegovina-Review-of-Efficiency-of-Services-in-Pre-University-Education-Phase-I-Stocktaking.pdf (accessed on 8 September 2020). [14]

Notes

[1] To account for differences in response style across countries and economies (e.g. if students from a country tend to respond more positively or negatively in general), OECD analysts adjusted the value of each individual index according to the average response across all indices.

[2] Since only one Western Balkan economy took the PISA teacher questionnaire in 2018, this paper does not discuss teachers' own experiences with ITE.

[3] Level of qualification refers to bachelor's degree, master's degree, or doctoral degree.

[4] Broadly speaking, education master's programmes are typically offered as either concurrent or consecutive models. Concurrent programmes provide pedagogical and practical training together with subject area knowledge, leading to a master's degree. Consecutive programmes organise pedagogical and practical training during the years of master's level studies, following the attainment of a bachelor's degree in a subject area.

[5] Sources of evidence for teacher appraisal may include classroom observations (often conducted by school principals) and reviews of teachers' lesson plans and classroom assessments (OECD, 2013[20]).

www.ingramcontent.com/pod-product-compliance
Ingram Content Group UK Ltd.
Pitfield, Milton Keynes, MK11 3LW, UK
UKHW050412240426
12048UKWH00020B/1477